The Service of Wisdom

The Service of Wisdom

The Focus of Dominican Life

Raimondo Spiazzi, OP

TRANSLATED BY
John Martin Ruiz, OP

FOREWORD BY
James Dominic Brent, OP

WIPF & STOCK · Eugene, Oregon

THE SERVICE OF WISDOM
The Focus of Dominican Life

Wipf & Stock
An Imprint of Wipf and Stock Publishers
199 W. 8th Ave., Suite 3
Eugene, OR 97401

www.wipfandstock.com

PAPERBACK ISBN: 978-1-6667-4967-0
HARDCOVER ISBN: 978-1-6667-4968-7
EBOOK ISBN: 978-1-6667-4969-4

10/04/22

"Wisdom looks at reality from God the Creator's point of view. In articulating the Dominican's love of wisdom, Spiazzi has also shown how even the laity can grow in holy wisdom."

—**Basil Cole**, OP, Dominican House of Studies

"In an age of confusion and chaos, this call to welcome the stabilizing dynamism of the Spirit of wisdom is both timely and needed. Notable in clarity and brevity, this book points to wisdom's source—the indwelling God whose creative, redemptive charity elevates and reorders our thoughts and lives. Anyone who hungers for the peace this world cannot give will find in this work an appetizing invitation to taste the sweet knowledge of eternal wisdom."

—**Mary Madeline Todd**, OP, Dominican Sisters of Saint Cecilia

"Seekers of truth and wisdom will be grateful for this translation of Fr. Spiazzi's wonderful little book *Il culto della Sapienza*. I recommend to anyone interested not just in a life of technical know-how, but in a life of that Wisdom which orders the universe to get their hands on this little book. Wisdom rewards those who pursue her."

—**Joseph-Mary Hertzog**, OP, Tangaza University College

"How often do we hear of Christian spirituality or consecrated life in terms of wisdom? Fr. Raimondo Spiazzi draws from his erudition and experience to show how the most lofty, necessary, and wondrous of callings is also the most universal and human— to serve at the sacred banquet of divine wisdom. This little book offers sumptuous fare for the mind and heart."

—**Bruno M. Shah**, OP, Providence College

"Reflecting the best of the Dominican theological tradition, Fr. Raimondo Spiazzi unfolds the place of wisdom in the spiritual life and how the gift of wisdom informs both contemplation and action. *The Service of Wisdom* has much to offer, not merely for the wise, but especially for those who wish to become so. Fr. John Martin Ruiz has provided a worthy English translation. I hope it will be widely read."

—**Gregory Schnakenberg**, OP, Dominican House of Studies

Contents

Translator's Note by John Martin Ruiz, OP | vii

Foreword by James Dominic Brent, OP | ix

Introduction | xi

Abbreviations | xv

Chapter 1: The Beginning of Wisdom | 1

Chapter 2: The Psychology of Wisdom | 7

Chapter 3: The Dynamism of Wisdom | 11

Chapter 4: The Denial of Wisdom | 14

Chapter 5: The Degrees of Wisdom | 17

Chapter 6: The Beatitude of Wisdom | 21

Chapter 7: The Asceticism of Wisdom | 24

Chapter 8: The Primacy of Wisdom | 29

Chapter 9: The Sins against Wisdom | 32

Chapter 10: Wisdom in Religious Life | 36

Chapter 11: Religious Vows as Paths of Wisdom | 40

Chapter 12: Wisdom and Prayer | 45

Chapter 13: Wisdom and the Sacraments | 50

Chapter 14: The Seat of Wisdom | 54

Chapter 15: The Bridegroom of Wisdom | 58

Chapter 16: From Beatitudes to Beatitude | 63

Bibliography | 71

Translator's Note

THIS BOOK IS A translation of *Il culto della Sapienza* by an Italian Dominican theologian Fr. Raimondo Spiazzi, OP (1918–2002). The Italian text was originally published in 1969, and the translation has adapted Fr. Spiazzi's original in small ways. For example, a couple of topical allusions to the purpose of the work as part of the "Alta Vena" series have been omitted, and I have added some supplementary footnotes that may be of interest to the reader. The translator's footnotes will be marked out as such.

All quotations from the *Summa Theologiae* are based on the Fathers of the English Dominican Province translation, which I frequently modify. The edition used is: Thomas Aquinas, *Summa Theologica: First Complete American edition*, literally translated by Fathers of the English Dominican Province through Benziger in 1947. Now there are indications that, at times, Fr. Spiazzi quotes some Italian translation of the *Summa Theologiae*. In such cases, I simply translated these Italian translations of the *Summa Theologiae* into English.

Please note that I have tried to give as faithful a representation as possible of the author's tone and meaning.

I am grateful to Fr. Fausto Arici, OP, former Prior Provincial of the Province of San Domenico in Italy, for granting permission to the Dominican Fathers of the Province of St. Joseph (USA) to publish this English translation.

Finally, I am especially grateful to Fr. Hugh Vincent Dyer, OP, Fr. Bruno Shah, OP, Fr. James Dominic Brent, OP, and the editors of Wipf & Stock for their encouragement, corrections, and suggestions to improve the translation.

John Martin Ruiz, OP
Dominican House of Studies
Washington, DC

Foreword

AMONG THE ANCIENTS IT was common to speak in awe of *Wisdom*, and to say things like "a multitude of wise men is the salvation of the world" (Wis 6:24). Though such discourse is now routinely dismissed as quaint, Father Spiazzi maintains that the graceful love of Wisdom—even the worship of Wisdom—is the distinctive focus of Dominican life. The grace of Saint Dominic is a special participation in eternal Wisdom, and his charism is "to communicate Wisdom with joy." Saint Dominic's followers share in his grace and charism, so Dominicans are devotees, servants, friends, lovers, spouses, worshippers, preachers, and teachers of the eternal and incarnate Wisdom of God. Under the influence of divine grace, Wisdom is both the one whom we serve and the one by whom we serve.

The Dominican form of life is one of prayer and study in fraternal communion for the sake of preaching for the salvation of souls. Father Spiazzi offers a theological explanation of our form of life. The Wisdom who set about creating the world is now set about saving the world in Jesus Christ. For he is the Wisdom of God, and it pleases Jesus Christ to include others in his work of salvation. First, he drew the twelve apostles into the work, and by his grace made them preachers of "the manifold wisdom of God" (Eph 3:10). Later, he drew Saint Dominic into it also as a preacher, and by grace made him "freely to pour forth the waters of wisdom."

Through no merit of our own, the grace and charism of Saint Dominic has now come to us, so that we too might share in the works of Wisdom. Our service of Wisdom consists of preaching the gospel of grace. Yet to do so in the manner of Saint Dominic, one needs a form of life composed of a harmonious balance of prayer, study, common life, apostolic intent, the vows, the liturgy, and the sacraments of the Church. Interiorly, one needs to form a tight integration of the three wisdoms: philosophical, theological, and mystical. To say how it all comes together in the service of Wisdom is the point of Father Spiazzi's book.

Translated literally, but inappropriately, the Italian title is "the cult to wisdom." In the contemporary context, the word "cult" arouses terror. In English, it now normally signifies a group of people, usually a religious group, whose minds have come under domination by an influential but pathological individual. In the classical sense, however, it means a ritual form of devotion, adoration, worship. The word *cultus* stands for something at once both communal and interior. It is both a group of people outwardly worshipping together *and* the free movements of their hearts. It is a common action in which personal love and service of God come alive. For this reason, the translation that best captures the meaning of the Italian title and, if Father Spiazzi is right, the phrase that best expresses the Dominican heart, is simply *The Service of Wisdom.*

Father James Dominic Brent, O.P.
The Pontifical Faculty of the Immaculate Conception at
The Dominican House of Studies
Washington, D.C.

Introduction

WHOEVER BECOMES A DOMINICAN does not look for Thebes in the Order.[1] He knows he is not entering the Grand Chartreuse, La Trappe Abbey, or the Camaldolese. His path does not go up to the Verna and does not go down to Manresa.[2] Only in certain cases of very personal callings and charisms, or at certain times in religious life (such as the novitiate, annual retreats, periods of rest), does the Dominican sit at the banquet of solitude. Normally, he is called to marriage with Wisdom in a contemplative life that does not necessarily require solitude as a permanent state, nor does it take place in the desert or in the hermitage. Rather, it takes place in the convent, which, as the word con-ventus ("agree," "assembly," "combine,") itself means, is a meeting place: a cloister, yes,

1. The author has in mind Thebes as an important Christian monastic location in Egypt. For the significance of Thebes in Egyptian monasticism, see Somida Awad, "Monastic," 48–57; Brooks, "Archeology," 665–84.—Trans.

2. The Verna is in reference to a Franciscan Sanctuary in Tuscany. According to Roest, Thomas of Celano's *Vita prima sancti Francisci* describes how St. Francis of Assisi received the stigmata during a "mountain retreat" on Monte La Verna. Roest, "Franciscan," 172. On the other hand, Manresa is a town in Spain. According to the account of his life, which he gave to Fr. Luis Gonçalves de Cámara, in March of 1522 St. Ignatius of Loyola went from Montserrat down to Manresa, where he spent some time praying, and had a mystical experience. See Dalmases, *Obras*, 101–109; Jackson, "Manresa," 1.—Trans.

but open to the sky high above while stretching out horizontally toward the way of the apostolate.

Dominican spirituality can therefore be conceived of and realized as a service to Wisdom. It is a spousal service, like that of St. Francis to Lady Poverty. The Dominican, like his founder and father, is rather the bridegroom of Lady Truth: but of the living Truth, of the eternal Word made flesh, Christ. Dominican life can be conceived of as a service to eternal Wisdom, as Blessed Henry Suso used to say. It is a service that is an exquisitely religious act (*famulatus, famuli Dei*).³ We can also say: worship of Wisdom. But it includes research, love, desire, study, devotion, and self-giving.

The biblical texts about wisdom immediately come to mind. It is a divine gift superior to all other goods, a manifestation of the truth and goodness of God in the world, the bride with whom you willingly spend your life (Wis 7:9–12; 9:4–6, etc.).

At the same time, the voice of St. Paul gives a warning against the false wisdom of the world and exalts the "folly of the Cross" (1 Cor 1:17–27; 3:19), which the apostles are sent to preach. These are the apostles of the early days and also those who over the centuries will take up their work as "vicars of Christ" (vicars of your work), agents of the Word. Saint Dominic is among these. He, who, as Saint Catherine says, had the responsibility of the Word. In fact in the liturgy of his feast, the first reading of the first Nocturne is the passage from the letter to the Corinthians on the "folly of the Cross." It seems like a call to the Dominican, so that he knows what to look for, what to choose, what to do, what to preach, if he wants to achieve the good and avoid wandering, as Dante says of the Order: "whereon one thriveth well if go not astray."⁴

The premise for possessing true wisdom, and overcoming the true folly through which too often we "wander," is to become childlike before God and men in order to receive, as Jesus says, the revelation of the Father (Matt 11:25), and, as St. Paul says, in order to recognize his truth, his light (See 1 Cor 2:6 ff; 3:18; 2 Cor 1:12; Rom 1:22; Eph 1:17; Col 1:9; 3:16). It is a matter of

3. "The service of God's servants." Rule, *Missal*, lxiii–lxv.—Trans.
4. Dante, *Paradiso*, 115.—Trans.

ceasing to be wise according to the world and of becoming wise according to God.

This turning to true wisdom, the wisdom of the Cross, includes the work of man, who must be attentive, docile, and faithful. But above all, it is the work of the Holy Spirit, eternal love, who leads to the secrets of eternal wisdom and to the heart of Christ, where the treasures of God's wisdom are gathered (Col 2:3).

If it is the Spirit who prays and groans in the Christian (Rom 8:26), it is also the Spirit who instills the search, the desire, the impulse towards the light in the Dominican soul. Thus, if the Dominican is a religious in dialogue with the truth, that is the Christ—truth of God, he is so in the Spirit and through the Spirit, who acts in the soul through the gift of wisdom. This is the grace to ask for with greater insistence.

> Da mihi sedium tuarum assistricem sapientiam . . .

> Give me Wisdom, the consort at your throne,
> And do not reject me from among your children;
> For I am your servant, the child of your maidservant,
> a man weak and short-lived
> and lacking in comprehension of judgment and of laws.
> Indeed, though one be perfect among mortals,
> if Wisdom, who comes from you, be lacking,
> that one will count for nothing (Wis 9:4–6).

The people from Ciociaria say in their customary prayer to St. Thomas Aquinas: "grant me the grace to keep also my good sense even when I am old."[5] That is to say, grant me the grace of not losing the use of reason, or, as they say, the senses. In the spiritual life, it deals with the understanding of God, which is given by wisdom.

---

5. According to Carle Zimmerman, "the *Ciociari* are people who wear a *ciocie*, which is a type of shoe similar to the Roman sandal . . . Ciociaria is not a geo-physical unit but a region in which the people called Ciociari are considerably interspersed at the extremities with other peoples . . . Among Italians, the Ciociari are known as robust people dedicated to the careful cultivation of their fields." Zimmerman, "Roots," 97.—Trans.

This is the gift to desire and to ask for. This is the greatest grace to which to aspire, as the wise one of the Old Testament teaches us:

Optavi, et datus est mihi sensus, et venit in me spiritus sapientae . . . [6]

> Therefore I prayed, and prudence was given me;
> I pleaded and the spirit of Wisdom came to me.
> I preferred her to scepter and throne,
> And deemed riches nothing in comparison with her,
> Beyond health and beauty I loved her,
> And I chose to have her rather than the light,
> because her radiance never ceases (Wis 7:7–8, 10).

Optavi: here is a word to set well in the heart as the root of all the dynamism of the spiritual life (See footnote no. 6).

The following pages present the broad lines of development of this dynamism, as a path to perfection followed precisely in the worship of wisdom.

It will be easy for the reader to notice that this book contains almost only notes that the author developed for a course of spiritual exercises carried out for a Dominican community in a small gothic world, of which he cherishes a sweet memory.[7]

Please bear in mind this fact: these pages have been written to offer a modest help (nothing more) to the "little ones" who seek the kingdom of God especially in the "wisdom of the heart."

6. P.G.W.Glare indicates that the main sense for Opto: Optare, Optavi, Optatum is "To express a wish for, desire, pray for." Glare, "Opto," 1260. Here *Optavi* has the sense of a pleading prayer, which is important for Fr. Spiazzi. He unfolds this concept throughout the book.—Trans.

7. Here he refers to the architecture but also to the forms of religious life of the Middle Ages, the language the prayer, the habit, etc.—Trans.

Abbreviations

Scripture:

Gen	Genesis
Exod	Exodus
Ps	Psalms
Prov	Proverbs
Eccl	Ecclesiastes
Wis	Wisdom
Matt	Matthew
Mark	Mark
Luke	Luke
John	John
Rom	Romans
1–2 Cor	1–2 Corinthians
Gal	Galatians
Eph	Ephesians
Col	Colossians
1–2 Thess	1–2 Thessalonians
Jas	James
1–2–3 John	1–2–3 John

Works of St. Thomas Aquinas:

DV	*Questiones Disputate De Veritate*
SG	*Summa Contra Gentiles*
ST	*Summa Theologiae*

Other:

OLD	*Oxford Latin Dictionary*

Chapter 1

The Beginning of Wisdom

WISDOM IS THE VIRTUE of order. According to the classical con-cept, the wise one is a man of order and the creator of order, either in the field of thought or in practical life. *Sapientis est ordi-nare.*[1] In this, perhaps, the wise man differs from the genius and the hero: the other two are human pinnacles, without a doubt, but they are generally characterized by the strong accentuation of an aspect of their personality, either the faculty of intuition and discovery, or the strength and courage of major exploits, but not without defect and dissonance altogether.

The saint, on the other hand, is the wise man who orders everything in his life to God and is inspired by a supernatural ge-nius, and he is capable of heroism, forged especially with wisdom through adversity, which gives him originality, without deforming the harmony of his personality. We see this whether it is the case of St. Francis of Assisi, St. Catherine of Siena, or St. Philip Neri.

Some saints stand out for their orderly wisdom of thought and action, rich in genius and expressed in heroism. These include St. Dominic and St. Thomas Aquinas. But later we will resume the conversation about them.

It is true, however, that the discussions of order and there-fore wisdom seem rather lacking today. According to Sedlmayr, our time is characterized by the loss of the center, not only in

1. *ST*, II–II, q. 45, a. 1: "The wise man sets in order all things."

architecture, but also generally in culture and in life.[2] Today, wisdom and order get a hearing, but strange men have taken them up. Some genuinely confused persons have become the heads of the peoples, and have decided the fate of millions of men. Even in the religious sphere and in the Church, for some time, a certain number of bewildered people, often in the guise of prophets or bearers of other charisms (and perhaps they are), are successful here and there. However, usually the charismatic ones, whether sacred or profane, ecclesiastical or political, if they are not saints, disrupt many things and do not build anything. Then again, in some cases, even a hurricane or an earthquake may be providential. Nevertheless, it is not easy to discern the signs, or even trace and see the paths of this providence. It is not permissible, for any reason, to fill the world with chatter.

The wise man builds in order. This does not mean unwillingness to accept change, or laziness, or absence of dynamism and courage, as is sometimes believed to be written on the wise man's clinical folder. St. Thomas Aquinas certainly did not err in this sense. He was a daring builder and an indomitable fighter, even if you cannot discern in his works or his life the sign of some imbalance.

What is most noticeable in the saints is equilibrium: the *ordo rationis* (order of reason) of virtue brought to a heroic climax. It is an ethical and ascetic balance that remedies even certain variations that can be found in the basic psyche of their personality. It is the strong affirmation of order that creates this balance. And the order is strong, stable, and consistent when it is structured around a principle capable of sustaining and vitalizing the whole organization. For the saint, this principle is the living God. For the wise Christian, God is the highest cause of all things.[3]

God is the first principle and the last end of everything, even of personality. He is the root of its dynamism, the eternal source from which everything flows and to which everything returns.

2. Hans Sedlmayr (1896–1984) was an Austrian art historian. See Sedlmayr, *Art*.—Trans.

3. *ST*, II-II, q. 45, a. 1; cf. *ST*, I-II, q. 57, a. 2.

God is, hence, the principle of the cosmological and ontological order: "*rerum Deus tenax vigor*"[4] and as such, he is the object of study and contemplation. God is the principle of the anthropological order and of the ethical order; and as such, he is the supreme law, transcendent exemplar ("be perfect, just as your heavenly Father is perfect," Matt 5:48), and the force of love that is attractive and unitive throughout human life.

It is about going up to him on the paths of wisdom, which gives rise to ascending order and dynamism in thought and in life.

It is, first of all, a question of knowing him, this God, principle and end.

For this purpose, a first path is needed: that of rational human wisdom, which on the scientific level becomes objectivized in metaphysics and within the inner life is identified with the subjective virtue of wisdom, the highest among the intellectual virtues,[5] which carries in itself something eternal because of the supreme and infinite things to which it refers.[6] The intellectual life is not complete except in wisdom. The sciences themselves are unrelated and incomplete until they fall into the superior synthesis of metaphysics, illuminator and corroborator of their principles, guarantor of the goodness of their conclusions in relation to the supreme demands of thought and life. A culture is always fragmentary and weak if it is not rooted in intellectual wisdom, and if it does not receive a unitary order from metaphysics.

Christian wisdom perfects human wisdom. It is a higher and safer way to God. This is theology as an objective doctrine developed by the data of revelation and as a subjective habit rooted in faith and acquired through study and reflection around divine truth. This is the first form of participation in the wisdom

4. According to Matthew Britt, this line is the title of an old hymn of the Roman breviary for the office of None, and it is attributed to St. Ambrose. It was translated by Rev. John Ellerton (1826–93) and Rev. Fenton J.A. Hort (1828–92) as "O Strength and Stay upholding all creation." Britt, *Hymns*, 37–38 and 365–67. The line could also be translated as "O God steadfast strength of all things."—Trans.

5. *ST*, I–II, q. 66, a. 5.

6. Cf. *ST*, I–II, q. 67, a. 2.

of God in those who have the ability and vocation for the study of his mystery.

Not all Christians are called to this, because few have the qualities, the time, and the inclination to become theologians on the scientific level. But there is a kind of nuclear and synthetic theology, which consists of an intuitive, savory, living knowledge of God. It is the wisdom that, as St. James says, "is from above" (Jas 3:17). It is a gift that is different both from faith, which it improves, as well as from wisdom as an intellectual virtue, which it transcends, and from all other intellectual and moral virtues that have as their object the means to reach the ultimate goal of human life. But supernatural wisdom, infused in the soul by the Holy Spirit, introduces the mind and heart into the intimate reality of God. It is not ratiocination and syllogistic knowledge, but affective, intuitive, and perceptive. It is actuated in the new affinity that exists between the soul and God by virtue of love: knowledge *per connaturalitatem*,[7] says St. Thomas.[8] Out of sympathy, Bergson would say.

It is the gift of which, as a Christian, one can say much more than the sacred writer of the Old Testament: *Venit in me spiritus sapientiae* (Wis 7:7).

This wisdom does not exclude human wisdom. Indeed, it requires it in the degrees and forms that are demanded for the vocation and duty of each person.

So, for the Dominican, the study of theology and philosophy is required, learning is required, and the scientific ordering of all the acquisitions of reason around the first principle, God, is required. It is God whom one discovers, contemplates, and adores as

7. Jacques Maritain defines connatural knowledge as "a kind of knowledge which is produced in the intellect but not by virtue of conceptual connections and by way of demonstration . . . But it is really and genuinely knowledge, though obscure and perhaps incapable of giving account of itself, or of being translated into words." Maritain, "Knowledge," 473–74.—Trans.

8. *ST*, II–II, q. 45, a. 4: "*Sapientia quae est donum Spiritus Sancti . . . facit rectitudinem iudicii circa res divinas, vel per regulas divinas de aliis, ex quadam connaturalitate sive unione ad divina. Quae quidem est per caritatem.*" Cf. *ST*, II–II, q. 45, a. 2.

One existing infinite absolute, eternal, most perfect, holy of holies, present and provident. It is theology carried out in what would be called the Prima Primae Partis of the *Summa* of St. Thomas. But it is also, in a supernatural key, as Father, Son, Holy Spirit, creative and redemptive charity, which is a divine name far deeper than philosophical ones, like the First Mover or First Cause of Aristotle, and of the same concept of subsisting Being already formulated in the Old Testament: "*Ego sum qui sum*" (Exod 3:14). The formally theological divine names (those of the Secunda Primae, so to speak, of St. Thomas) and especially that of Charity (which the Tertia Pars develops) allow theological wisdom to realize a new and perfect dimension of the knowledge and preaching of God.

With the orderly exercise of this knowledge, one can easily form a theological mindset that is reflected in all of one's existence. It is reproduced in thought as an ordering synthesis and theocentric vision of the world, of life, and of history; and it is emulated in virtues and behavior, as a reference to God beginning and end, from which the true *ordo rationis* derives. It is also manifested in piety and contemplation, in which the spirit of God acts more than the spirit of man (Rom 8:26–27) and everything feels, judges, and works according to the mind of Christ: "But we have the mind of Christ" (1 Cor 2:16).

Here the wisdom infused as a gift of the Holy Spirit fits as a grafting point. This gift perfects theology, small or large, developed by faith. It also revives and fertilizes the notions learned from the catechism, from the readings and from the study that each can and must do according to his state. It often provides for the lack of theology and a catechism.

This gift gives the soul the "right judgment about divine things" and the capacity for an immediate reference of everything to God, in thought and in life.

On the ethical level, this right judgment about divine things immediately translates into an attitude of piety and fear, which is characteristic of the truly religious soul, of the "*vir iustus,*" of a man who has become a child of God.[9]

9. *ST*, II–II, q. 45, a. 1, ad 3.

"The fear of the Lord is beginning of wisdom" (Ps 111:10; Eccl 1:16). Here begins the path of humility, spiritual childhood, which through study, contemplation, and love leads to the possession of God and to the taste of his truth in wisdom.

Chapter 2

The Psychology of Wisdom

WHEN WE PRESENT WISDOM as a synthesis of spirituality, it is easy to appear as conceited or presumptuous intellectuals, as men more apt to analyze than to love and serve God in simplicity of heart (Wis 1:1).

The risk of the theological profession is that one can become a rationalist in thought and in life. But theology is not true if it is overly cerebral, and spirituality cannot be nourished by rationalism. Theology is born of faith and lives by faith. Spirituality is a theory and a method of communion with the living God. Even when spirituality has its foundation in wisdom, it cannot be conceived of and classified as intellectualism, because wisdom is a gift of the Holy Spirit that, if it is infused in the intellect as in its connatural seat, is rooted in love and tends towards love.

For this reason, St. Catherine of Siena, speaking of the way of life God assigned to St. Dominic, speaks of knowledge (or wisdom), but she immediately adds that it is a knowledge that is learned and distributed at the table of the cross. This is the Dominican banquet that surpasses and integrates the Platonic and Dantean one.[1] And it is therefore a science and a preaching of the cross for the salvation of souls.

---

1. Here the author is referring to the most holy Eucharist in general but also to a specific phrase from the Office and Mass for the feast of Corpus Christi written by St. Thomas Aquinas. This phrase is now used as the antiphon of the

St. Thomas Aquinas confirms the primacy of love over knowledge of God in this life. He notes that knowledge reduces God to the measure of man by conceiving him according to the analogies taken from things. Love, on the other hand, is a going out of the soul, of the self, to enter into God and live in communion with him, possessed, recognized, and almost felt as he is.

And St. Thomas also describes a psychology of wisdom that allows us to discover its fullness of meaning as a function of the spiritual life.

St. Thomas argues that, subjectively, wisdom is essentially necessary for a right judgment about divine things. Now this judgment can be made according to a perfect use of reason, and if one has the intellectual virtue of wisdom which presides over metaphysics and theology. This judgment can be made according to a certain connaturality with the matter at hand. For example, this happens in a chaste soul that, in a vital way and not only rationally and speculatively, judges in matters of chastity. A finely tuned conscience often radiates with chastity, giving the intellectual faculty the ability to see the distinction between good and evil in this realm. In addition, the judgment can be made in those who have a supernatural power to feel and to judge divine things by a certain connaturality, or "compassion," or "sympathy," created by love.

Wisdom as a gift of the Spirit is precisely this faculty of judgment that is given and is exercised in the strength of charity. Therefore, one can say that wisdom is essentially an intellectual gift because the faculty of judgment is the intellect, but it is rooted in love and therefore engages the faculty of love. That is to say, it engages the will, or better said the heart.[2] "*Sapientia cordis*" (Wisdom of the heart*)*, as John XXIII once said.

Charity is the essence of Christian perfection as a participation in the soul of the very love of God, or as St. Thomas says,

---

Magnificat at Evening Prayer II in the Liturgy of the Hours. Dominicans pray this antiphon every day, in adoration of the Blessed Sacrament: "*O sacrum convivium, in quo Christus sumitur: recolitur memoria passionis eius, mens impletur gratia et futurae gloriae nobis pignus datur.*" *Liturgia*, 542.—Trans.

2. *ST*, II–II, q. 45, a. 2.

of the Holy Spirit.[3] Charity in us is a certain participation of the Holy Spirit.

Charity unites the soul to God in friendship, and thus it creates an atmosphere of love in which the soul knows God intimately almost from within and not making an effort as in pure rational knowledge. But charity, which vivifies faith, inspires and penetrates the depths of theology as research and reflection about the truths of faith, and it gives a new fundamental value even to philosophy, to metaphysics, insofar as it is used in theology. Thus is realized in a superior way the unity of love—knowledge, thought—life, which is the ideal to which man tends by the very dynamism of his unitary nature.

The intellect perfected and enlivened by wisdom knows God in love. Perfected wisdom is true knowledge; and it can be true science, which is not to be disregarded or neglected, especially as it saves from sentimentalism and fanaticism to which pseudo–mystics and spiritual charlatans easily tend. But knowledge perfected by wisdom gives strength and seriousness to the spiritual life.

The intellect alone cannot arrive at total knowledge of God, or at the vital participation in the eternal procession of the Word, to become an image of the Image (name of the Word). In contrast, when penetrated by wisdom and enlivened by love, the intellect arrives not only at the knowledge but also at tasting "a certain sweetness" of God.[4]

One then has an experiential and joyful knowledge of God in the living Christ in the soul. This joyful knowledge is that apex of the spiritual life of which St. Thomas, following St. Augustine, writes:

> Whereas Son is the Word, not any sort of word, but one Who breathes forth love . . . Thus, the Son is sent not in accordance with every and any kind of intellectual perfection, but according to intellectual illumination, which breaks forth into the affection of love, as is said (in John 6:45): *Everyone that hath heard from the Father*

3. *ST*, II–II, q. 23, a. 3, ad 3; Cf. a. 2.
4. *ST*, II–II, q. 45, a. 2, ad 1.

and hath learned, cometh to Me . . . Thus, Augustine
plainly says (De Trin. iv, 20): "The Son is sent whenever
He is known and perceived by anyone." Now perception
implies a certain experimental knowledge, and this is
properly called *wisdom* [sapientia], as it were a sweet
knowledge [sapida scientia] . . . [5]

At the root of this new capacity to know is faith, in which the
activity of wisdom takes place. In addition, the gift of wisdom is
linked to the other two intellectual gifts: the gift of understanding,
which serves to perceive the sense of the truth believed; and the
gift of knowledge, which serves to judge every fact according to
the right views of the human spirit.[6] Wisdom, however, elevates
the whole psychology of knowledge and judgment, because divine
reasons prevail in everything. Those who live in wisdom, live according to the intimate thought of God.

5. *ST,* I, q. 43, a. 5, ad 2; cf. St Augustine, *De Trinitate,* IX, c. 10, ML. 42,
969. See *De Trinitate,* 306.—Trans.

6. Cf. *ST,* II–II, q. 45, a. 2, ad 3.

Chapter 3

The Dynamism of Wisdom

WHEN ONE HEARS OF someone who devotes himself to the worship of wisdom, it is easy to immediately think of a bookworm, or a lab rat, as they say; and even more so, it is easy to think of a person immersed in the way of ideas, abstracted from life, and impractical. It is the notion that some have about Dominicans here and there. Let's be honest, this view is sometimes justified by certain aspects of our life and of our organization, which do not shine with practicality. But mind you these are defective aspects, not only because of the relationship to the so-called practical spirit, but also because of the relationship to wisdom. They indicate that for some of us, not for the best or for our saints, knowledge remains in the clouds and does not descend into life and does not become wisdom.

In reality, supernatural wisdom is not abstract; and on the other hand, the practical is not empiricism, pragmatism, or activism. The contemplative life is not a sheer play of thought, as is seen in the story of the Seven Wise Men, or Socrates, Plato, and Aristotle in the Hellenic world, or Confucius and Lao-Tse in the East, etc. On the other hand, the active life, according to the classical concept, is not made of work without thought, or without prayer. Theoretical activity does not exclude practical activity; and the active life, the exercise of the moral virtues under the direction of prudence, does not exclude the light of a higher truth deepened and enjoyed in contemplation.

A single principle, a single faculty, presides over the twofold form of activity: the superior reason in the contemplation of the truths that transcend man, and the inferior reason in the reflection and in the decision on human actions. Man is not made of watertight compartments with the faculty of contemplation and the faculty of action, or intelligence and will, inner life and work. One spiritual faculty thinks and contemplates the great truths (*ratio superior*) and directs action (*ratio inferior*); the practical reason is not separate from the speculative or theoretical one; reason and will interpenetrate and influence each other in their activity.

The gift of wisdom is infused in the unity of the human spirit, and it prepares it for an activity that is at the same time contemplation of eternal things and direction of human things according to eternal things. It could be described as a thought that is knowledge of the truth but also intelligence of action.

Certainly the most important moment of the spiritual dynamism that develops from the gift of wisdom is the theoretical one, that is, the contemplation of God, the supreme object of wisdom. But it makes the light of eternal Truth pass into practice,[1] realizing the ideal of action emanating from contemplation, and, when it comes to the apostolate, of social communication of the truth, of "*contemplari et contemplata aliis tradere:*" the most perfect life.[2]

St. Dominic's passion for souls was ignited and burned in contemplating the plan of God who wants all of us to be saved by his creative and redemptive mercy, but with human, personal, and social collaboration. Knowing that God wanted him to be his minister in the work of salvation, he passed from contemplation to action, from love of God to love of neighbor, not by subtraction, but by expansion, effacing himself without impoverishing himself.

The gift of wisdom that worked in him was a source of life and not just of theory, like intellectual wisdom.[3]

---

1. Cf. *ST,* II–II, q. 45, a. 3, ad 2.

2. *ST,* II–II, q. 188, a. 6. : "For even as it is better to enlighten than merely to shine, so it is better to give to others the fruits of one's contemplation than merely to contemplate."

3. *ST,* II–II, q. 45, a. 3, ad 1.

Nevertheless, the gift of wisdom maintained the right proportions between the two moments, contemplative and active, and it welded the expressions in the single spiritual synthesis of Saint Dominic, to which his followers and companions testified during the process of canonization. They said he spoke only with God or about God.

In reality, the reference to God constituted for him the reason for both contemplation and action. But the gift of wisdom had more directly as its object the contemplation of God, the beginning and source of everything (*contemplatio divinorum, quae est visio principii*) and afterwards the direction of human acts according to the supreme reasons contemplated in God (*dirigere actus humanos secundum rationes divinas*).[4] Or rather, it directed according to the divine will, law, and plan.

Such is the meaning of Christian contemplation.

Thus one cannot pose a humanism of action against an asceticism or spirituality of contemplation, because what matters most is not the form of activity to which one devotes oneself according to capacity, vocation, fortune, etc., but reference to the divine reasons.[5]

The gift of wisdom establishes the connection with these reasons and always lets them triumph in life. By the gift of wisdom, the action becomes sweet and work restful,[6] almost in advance of the eternal "Sabbath."

Therefore, we can understand that proclamation of the sequence of Pentecost addressed to the Holy Spirit:

> Rest in labor, coolness sweet
> Tempering the burning heat
> Truest comfort of our woes.[7]

---

4. *ST*, II–II, q. 45, a. 3.

5. *ST*, II–II, q. 45, a. 3, ad 3.

6. *ST*, II–II, q. 45, a. 3, ad 3.

7. Britt shows that this is from the Feast of Pentecost in the Roman Missal, and it is a translation by Fr. James Ambrose Aylward, OP (1813–72): "In labore requies, in aestu temperies, in fletu solatium." Britt, *Hymns*, 160 and 362.—Trans.

Chapter 4

The Denial of Wisdom

Wisdom, as a gift of the Holy Spirit, is rooted in charity, which gives the human spirit connaturality with the divine Spirit. And charity is grace; it is a current of grace towards God.

Sin, which by definition is the breaking of friendship with God, takes away charity and grace and causes the gift of wisdom to be lost. Without grace there is no wisdom.[1] The latter is a thesis of St. Thomas, so obvious and persuasive. It contains a serious warning to those who dedicate themselves by vocation, and almost by profession, to the worship of wisdom.

Some can be learned, wise, and very knowledgeable according to the judgment of the world, according to public opinion and perhaps even in the reality of the knowledge they possess, but without charity, without grace, they are not wise according to God. They can be great men, but they are not truly wise.

Sin also has this character of ignorance, which fosters negativity. Being disobedience to God, the author of goodness, truth, and law, ignorance is a pretense to attribute to oneself "the knowledge of good and evil," as Adam and Eve did in the biblical story (Gen 3:5). In other words, the sinner attributes to himself the judgment on the value of actions, the faculty to determine good and evil, and the mastery over the moral order.

---

1. *ST,* II–II, q. 45, a. 4.

The true judge of good and evil can only be the one who is the author of the law; and the author of the law can only be the creator of man and of everything, namely God. It is therefore an ignorance, even before an arrogant pretension, to replace God for the "knowledge of good and evil," and to proclaim with Nietzsche the "death of God" to replace his law with the law of man or of the superman. It is an ignorance to claim absolute autonomy of man as reason and freedom before God and in the name of this autonomy to choose atheism.

This ignorance is found to a greater or lesser extent in every sin. Every sinner tries to take God's place in the moral order when he chooses what he pleases and not what is due in response to the demands of God's law.

In every sin, there is an inversion of values: no longer is the judgment on everything in relation to divine things, to the supreme cause, that is, to God as in wisdom, but there is the subordination of everything, even of the relationship with God, to a fancy, a feeling, a will, which depends on inferior motives. Heaven is postponed for the satisfaction of a pleasure or a vanity, and a handful of dust is preferred to the grace of God. Such is the ignorance of sin.

The Holy Spirit gives wisdom, which is the principle of order. Sin produces *disorder*, which is the fruit of ignorance.

From the theological point of view, disorder consists in disobedience and is virtually a rebellion against God who is the first principle of universal order.

From the psychological point of view, disorder consists in this sort of internal overturning of man, whereby the lower part prevails on the upper part, the passions on the will, feelings on reason, the flesh on the spirit, and nature on grace. It is a human failure that deserves that judgment that is both commiseration, mercy, and irony that the Bible puts in God's mouth: "See! The man has become like one of us" (Gen 3:22).

Being like God: this is the dream of the eternal Adam who lives in every man. To be reduced to failure and the imbalance of human nature is a reality that is experienced every day. Between dream and reality, as in the first sin, there is always an act of madness and ignorance.

The choice between wisdom and ignorance is presented to man in every hour of his life, or rather, a choice between the wisdom of the Spirit and the wisdom of the flesh, between the law of God and the "philosophy of the serpent" that promises: you will be like gods (Gen 3:5).

One can pretend to be like God in the usurpation of his prerogatives, of his attributes, and this is the ignorance that loses. One can aspire to be like God in the participation of his nature and his life through his grace, in the connaturality with him realized in charity; and this is the wisdom that gives true light to see, a true heart to love, and true strength to reach perfection.

It is therefore around wisdom that the great struggle takes place, both inside and outside of man. It is there that the boundary dividing "the children of perdition from the children of the kingdom" arises (John 17:12; 2 Thess 2:3; Rom 8:17–9:8).[2]

2. *ST*, II–II, q. 45, a. 4, ad 3.

Chapter 5

The Degrees of Wisdom

THE GIFTS OF THE Holy Spirit are in all souls in the state of grace since baptism. They are part of the Christian's supernatural endowments; they are jewels. Even the gift of wisdom is in all the baptized. If it is not lost as a result of sin, it is at the root of all contemplation and practical wisdom.

In fact, the gift of wisdom infuses in the soul the right judgment about divine things, both contemplated in their truths and accepted and embraced as the light of action. This gift gives "certain rectitude of judgment in the contemplation and consultation of Divine things."[1]

But there are varying degrees of participation in the divine truth, which is foundational for this sapiential judgment, as there are varying degrees of union with God in charity and of possession of his grace.

It is true that all the baptized Christians living in grace should themselves be wise. This is their vocation. But human reality is complex and often intricate, and it affects the whole life of grace, and even life in wisdom.

Physical and psychic conditions, moods, complexes, mentality, social pressures, and stronger personality influences, etc., constitute a set of factors, which, in concrete personal existence, favors

1. *ST,* II–II, q. 45, a. 5.

or hinders, according to each case, the development of the seed of grace and wisdom deposited in all with baptism.

We must also say that not everyone has the same qualities and abilities, nor the same charisms, or the same mission and function in the Church and in the world. Therefore, different particular vocations correspond to different measures of divine gifts, different degrees of grace, charity, and wisdom.

It can be said that all those who have sanctifying grace (*gratum faciens*) participate in the right judgment of the Holy Spirit, in wisdom, in the whole sphere of the demands of eternal salvation, both in contemplation, in prayer, in the interior life, and in the good ordering of human things according to the norms of divine law.

The wisdom of good Christians often translates and reveals itself in those forms of Christian common sense which stands out in holy souls, even when they are of humble condition and of little culture.

Here are three examples. First, an old mother, an ordinary woman, replied to someone who exalted before her the success of her son: "Sarah, but it seems to me that things are going too well for him. I do not know if this is his true good." Second, an old religious, hearing someone praising a young confrere who did not dare to ask the superior what he needed, observed, "It seems to me that the friar lacks humility, because, in a religious, humility must come to the point of revealing his own needs to the superior with simplicity and ask for his help." Third, another religious who was a Dominican cooperator brother for many years, upon hearing that a common exercise of piety had been suppressed in the convent, simply remarked, "It seems to me that these are times when prayer must be increased, not abolished."

The root of the "right judgment" of wisdom is sanctifying grace, which is a participation in the divine nature and life. But it is conveyed and made to flourish in the soul by a present grace; that is, by a motion, an impulse of the Holy Spirit that drives man to perform salutary works. The Holy Spirit moves men towards the good and the search for God, to prayer, to study, and to exercise all the virtues. "But his anointing teaches you about everything," St. John used to say to Christians (1 John 2:27).

It is the teaching that is given to everyone by the inner master who dwells in the soul, namely God. It is a question of listening to him, of following him, and, indeed before that, of lending an ear, of making the heart ready and docile to his word.

Nevertheless, whoever has grace can be sure that the light of the Spirit does not fail in the things necessary for salvation; just as in the things necessary for life, the nature of his spontaneous movement of affirmation and protection does not fail. All souls in the state of grace have in themselves sufficient strength to live in wisdom. All Christians can and are called to be wise.

It is clear, however, that various degrees of wisdom are implemented in the measure of charity and adherence to the "intelligible principle," that is, to the first truth, to God who is the light of life. The highest degree is that of those who are better acquainted with the even deeper divine mysteries ("knowledge of the mysteries of the kingdom of God has been granted to you . . . " Luke 8:10), which they can make known to others; and that together, they know not only how to direct themselves according to the divine norms but also others. These are the wise par excellence, the ones who even in the common opinion are often recognized as such.

Please note that they are not the purely speculative minds but the incisive connoisseurs of the mystery, so good connoisseurs, so as to know how to communicate knowledge. They are not only professors or scholars of abstract thought but the teachers of life. They are not only the theoreticians, but they are also the wise ones who know how to give the right order to life itself, and, in the form of counsel, exhortation, and spiritual direction. The truly wise know how to exercise authority and governance, both on the life of individuals and of a community.

This degree of wisdom is not common to all. Indeed, it seems that it is rare.

In some who truly possess it, and whom we meet here and there, it is rather a grace gratis data, or a charism. It is one of those gifts that, according to St. Paul (1 Cor 12:8), the Holy Spirit distributes as he will according to the eternal purpose that assigns vocations and arranges the functions for the edification of the Church (Eph 4:12; 1 Cor 14:5; 14:26): now there is a gift of governance, now a gift of prophecy, now a gift of miracles, now a special gift of wisdom (word of wisdom) . . . [2]

This wisdom that was in Christ and in the apostles is the gift of "prelates," of superiors, of spiritual directors, and of all those who are called to build up the Church in minds and consciences.

St. Dominic and St. Catherine of Siena possessed this gift abundantly, and we can say it is the charism that stands out also in all the other Dominican saints.

Those who like the Dominican are called to instruct and direct others for salvation need this charism. To instruct and direct is a hierarchical action, but it must be accompanied by charisms, especially that of wisdom.

A certain prophetic impulse has always been in the Order of St. Dominic: from the founder to St. Catherine and from St. Vincent Ferrer to Savonarola and to Lacordaire, to certain pioneers of the current process of ecclesial renewal.

It is a heritage to be treasured and a mission to be developed, along the lines of ministry and in the light of wisdom. This is how Dominican spirituality is translated into an apostolate.

2. Cf. *ST,* II–II, q. 177, a. 1–2; q. 45, a. 5.

Chapter 6

The Beatitude of Wisdom

WITH SOME EFFORT BUT not without efficacy, St. Thomas seeks to match the gifts of the Holy Spirit with the beatitudes proclaimed by Jesus. He presents them as perfect acts of the virtues that have their productive instruments in their gifts. In this scheme, the beatitude of wisdom is that of peace: "Blessed are the peacemakers, for they will be called children of God" (Matt 5:9). Peace is the merit of beatitude; the divine sonship is the reward. Peace is the root. The divine sonship is the flower, and the fruit is eternal life.[1]

Certainly, the wise man possesses and gives peace. He is and feels himself a child of God, a member of his family and of his kingdom. St. Thomas himself is an example of this beatitude, with his soul full of peace, with that simplicity and transparency of a child of God.

In fact, wisdom makes the Christian an agent of peace, of that peace which is the tranquility of order, because the wise one creates order (sets things in order) and preserves it. To live in wisdom is to order oneself and others to the first principle, God, and to see everything, to judge, and to operate righteously in harmony with this principle in a constant and progressive way.

However, the peace that comes from the gift of wisdom is something intimate and profound that the world neither gives nor can take away (John 14:27). It is the peace of Christ, and

1. *ST,* II–II, q. 45, a. 6.

indeed it is Christ himself, *pax nostra* (Eph 2:14), who shares his own peace with the soul in which he lives. Christ is for the soul his possession of the divine good, stable, lasting and relished. This profound peace causes in the soul a serenity that remains even when, on the surface of life and human psychology itself, the sea seems rough or even tempestuous. It is because the Spirit, with the gift of wisdom, gives to the soul something of the eternal order in which God's own life take place that we attribute to him, among other names, also that of "Peace."[2]

When this true peace is in the Christian, he can become a dispenser and an architect of peace even outside of himself, in families and in communities, in the Church and in the world. He really is then one of those wise peacemakers that humanity needs, a bearer of peace, because he lives in wisdom.

His reward is a conscience that is full of life and a fuller enjoyment of divine sonship.

He is like a more perfect image of the Son of God, the incarnate Word who is formed in the soul and lives in wisdom and in peace, as a realization of the eternal predestination of the Father, by the work of the Holy Spirit.[3] As St. Paul says: "those he foreknew he also predestined to be conformed to the image of his Son" (Rom 8:29).

The Son of God is uncreated Wisdom, generated by the Father, and incarnate. Already in the Old Testament, the Bible makes this a lofty celebration. St. John, speaking of the Logos, or Word of God, better personalizes it and identifies it with Christ, the Word made flesh (John 1:1–14).

Jesus himself says that he comes with the Father and dwells in those who love him (John 14:23). He is the Logos, Wisdom.[4] He is the eternal principle of every truth and good that the Holy Spirit makes present in the soul with the gift of wisdom.

By virtue of this participation, the soul best reaches the likeness of the divine exemplar, until it reaches it as an end almost in

---

2. Cf. Pseudo-Dionysius the Areopagite, *De divinis nominibus*, ch. 11.

3. *ST*, III, q. 23, a. 2, ad 3.

4. *ST*, I, q. 39, a. 8.

an anticipation of the eternal possession. St. Thomas says that, for this reason, "by participating in the gift of wisdom, man attains to the sonship of God."[5]

It is an image realized in the mind, but as the supreme flowering of charity.[6]

The spirituality of those who dedicate themselves to the worship of wisdom and to the apostolate of wisdom differs from cold intellectualism! St. Thomas points out that if peace is in charity, it is wisdom rooted in charity that, in ordering the spiritual life and human conduct as a participation of the "intellectual light full of love" (as Dante would say), realizes this peace in charity.[7] "Lovers of your law have much peace" (Ps 119:165).

Nevertheless, the principle and source of charity is always the Holy Spirit, eternal Love that is present in the soul as love. In giving us the adoption of the children of God, this Spirit makes us talk with and pray to the Father, calling him and hearing him precisely as Abba, Father (Rom 8:15; Gal 4:6)!

It is the Spirit that moves us, makes us act, and guides us as children of God (Rom 8:14).

But it is in the gift of wisdom flourishing by charity that the Holy Spirit produces in the soul that resemblance to eternal Wisdom that makes us children of God. Therefore, the beatitude of peace and divine sonship is realized in wisdom vivified by love.

As the Bible says, Eternal Wisdom passing through the world produces friends of God and prophets (Wis 7:27). He is the Son of God, who by means of the Spirit unites men to himself in charity and intimately reveals to them the mysteries of the Father with infused wisdom. The latter is the effect of charity and the principle of peace and divine sonship in souls. This sonship is the ineffable beatitude of wisdom.

5. *ST,* II–II, q. 45, a. 6.

6. *ST,* II–II, q. 45, a. 6, ad 1.

7. *ST,* II–II, q. 45, a. 6, ad 1.

Chapter 7

The Asceticism of Wisdom

IN ORDER TO LIVE in wisdom and, above all, to reach the beatitude of wisdom, an inner and external discipline is indispensable. It is a discipline that subjugates passions, regulates actions, and gives balance to all being and harmony to one's life. In short, it takes asceticism.

The spirituality of wisdom does not exclude but requires the asceticism of the moral virtues precisely because, as the Bible says, in wisdom there must be no stain, no pollution of spurious and degrading elements. Nothing defiled can enter into her (Wis 7:25).

Wisdom matters to order: order in thought, in affections, in feelings, and in actions. St. Thomas insists upon affirming it: "It belongs to wisdom, as a gift, not only to contemplate Divine things, but also to regulate human acts."[1]

Asceticism is therefore a preparation for wisdom, and at the same time it is its effect, way and expansion, humus and flowering. Asceticism and wisdom have the same relationship that exists between the active and contemplative life. The first opens the way to the second and together receive from it a superior light and higher motivations.

Thus wisdom itself implies in its economy the whole ascetic life; and this, at least in a Thomistic and Dominican key, is incorporated into the program of spirituality which starts from the

1. *ST,* II–II, q. 45, a. 6, ad 3.

intent of contemplation and develops in wisdom to achieve it, without excluding the highest peaks of mysticism. On the whole of the ascetic and mystical way, the soul moves under the direction of the Spirit and becomes more and more passive as it grows in the degrees of wisdom.

Mysticism without the ascetic part would be illusory. In the spiritual life, it is indeed necessary to build the building of moral virtues under the guidance of prudence. The theological virtues themselves and the gifts of the Holy Spirit could not exist without the moral virtues. The moral virtues are preparation for it and the ground for insertion and practical reproof, at least in the subjects endowed with the use of reason (for children baptized before having reached the use of reason, there can be a mysterious dynamic of charity and the gifts, of which there are sometimes amazing revelations).

On the other hand, the practice of the moral virtues without the finality of wisdom, which is the possession, knowledge and taste of God, would resemble a construction without crowning and without basis. In Christianity, there is no mysticism without asceticism; and there is no asceticism without mysticism. The gift of wisdom with the light of contemplation also directs human acts and the practice of the moral virtues.

According to St. Thomas, the role of preparation for contemplation belongs in a particular way to certain virtues that contribute to giving wisdom the qualities that the Letter of St. James (3:17) attributes to it:

> "But the wisdom from above
> is first of all pure, then peaceable
> gentle, compliant,[agreeing with the good],[2]
> full of mercy and good fruits,
> without inconstancy or insincerity."

2. *Bonis consentiens* is a Latin phrase that is not translated by the *New American Bible*. But the author includes this phrase in the Italian text. So here I translated as: "agreeing with the good."—Trans.

According to St. James, one needs to appeal to these tests in order to judge if one has wisdom: "Who among you is wise and understanding? Let him show his works by a good life in the humility that comes from wisdom" (Jas 3:13).

While purely natural wisdom, which consists in the ability to know and speculate, can be true even without the moral virtues, Christian wisdom demands them as the substance of the spiritual life itself to which it gives origin and tone.

Thus, it unfolds before the mind all its richness of content, its totality.

Above all, wisdom is pure. St. Thomas explains this with the idea of the liberation from evil (*remotio a malis*), that is from sin, which is the negation of wisdom. Indeed: "the fear of the Lord is the beginning of wisdom" (Ps 111:10). Fear is the beginning of wisdom inasmuch as it leads away from evil, from sin. It may be the fear of the worldly sort, which is in reality dread of God. This does not enter into the economy of the spiritual life; it is in fact a sin. But there is a threefold form of fear of God that benefits the Christian: servile, filial, and reverential. The first is fear of God's punishments. The second is fear of offending him, and the third is fear of failing in his love, in a sense of reverence for his infinite majesty. The latter fear will last even in heaven; on earth, this kind of fear leads to seeking ever-greater purity. It is chaste fear for which wisdom can said to be pure. That is to say, it is the sum distance from moral evil, and it is spiritual transparency and luminosity. It is purity in a general sense, which also includes the purification from all concupiscence and especially from that of the flesh. But it goes far beyond, as the supreme triumph of the spirit of good in all life.

In addition, here are the other steps of the asceticism of wisdom, ordered to its end, which is the peace of the soul. The last of these steps is peace, aim and end of the sapiential—ascetic exercise: "then peaceable," says the Letter of St. James. St. Thomas says that "wisdom is peaceful," because "wherein lies the ultimate effect of wisdom, for which reason peace is numbered among the beatitudes . . . whereby all things are reduced to their right order; and it is this that constitutes peace."[3]

From "pure" to "peaceable:" this is the entire path to cover in the ascetic life in order to obtain the beatitude of wisdom and bring peace, after the soul has detached itself from sin by means of purity. First of all, those that respond to the need for proper moderation and balance, necessary in personal and social life, must show certain modesty in everything. They are those who with St. Catherine can be understood in one word: "discretion." It is the right means, the right order in all the virtues. It is the balance between opposing needs and sometimes between opposing extremes. It is the balance between modesty (=measure), intellectual humility, and modesty in feelings, affections, sensitivity, and actions.

But nobody is sufficient to himself in everything. In many things, you need advice and direction. Therefore, wisdom is "*suadibilis*," that is docile, easy to be persuaded, well-disposed to the truth, and open to dialogue. True wisdom, precisely because it is "*suadibilis*," excludes every obtuseness and obstinacy, every pride and bias, and leads instead to recognize the truth of others, to ask for their intellectual and moral help, to treasure their teaching, and follow the advice of others. The wise man is convinced that there is always something to learn from everyone, even the youngest ones, sometimes from them above all. He knows that we must seize and take advantage of all the opportunities offered by others to improve and make progress. He knows that social life, and especially common life, has mainly this function of serving for the salvation and perfection of anyone and everyone. Therefore, he accepts and respects it, makes use of it and contributes to it, even between trials and sorrows. Paratus semper doceri (always prepared to learn), was the motto of Cardinal Mercati, taken from the *Imitation of Christ*, and this motto was so dear even to our Father Cordovani.[4]

3. *ST*, II–II, q. 45, a. 6, ad 3.

4. Fr. Mariano Cordovani, OP (1883–1950) was a renowned Italian Dominican, theologian, and Thomist. For more on him see Molinaro, "Neoscolastica," 452.—Trans.

There is also a social asceticism whose first criterion is to recognize, love, esteem, praise, procure, and not envy the good of others. It is to allow others the good, to see this good, to interpret it as such, and to enjoy it, yielding to the good.

In the wise one there is no animus, but goodness, candor, delicacy, sweetness, clemency as in St. Dominic, even joviality and wit, as in St. Thomas.

It belongs to this spirit to be broad of mind and heart, generous, able to understand, to join others, to help them value the gifts received from the Lord: actually help his neighbor. That is to say, to bear good fruit (full of . . . good fruits). It also includes the ability to share defects: compassionate about his neighbor's needs in suffering . . . Because, as the Letter of St. James (3:17) says, wisdom is full of mercy, full of pity, and compassion. This does not mean connivance with evil, complicity, and silence. Wisdom practices fraternal correction, which is a work of charity: to strive in all charity to correct the faults of others. Charity never allows the truth to be betrayed, either in oneself or in relation to others. Wisdom leads to a sincere judgment, judging without dissimulation, but at the same time is benign and free from any influx of feelings and resentments (lest he should pretend to correct while really intending to carry out hatred).

It is a complete and linear ascetic program, and it is solid and transparent. This is the path traced for the soul that wants to live in wisdom. It begins with the fear of God and ends in peace: *per aspera ad astra, per crucem ad lucem.*[5]

---

5. This Latin phrase can be translated as "through hard conditions to the stars, through the cross to the light." Since the first part of the phrase is found in Virgil's *Aeneid*, among others, perhaps here the author is using it to allude to the ending of Dante's *Inferno* which says: "My leader [Virgil] then, and I, in order to regain the world of light, entered upon a dark and hidden path; and, without caring for repose, went up, he going ahead, and I behind, till through a rounded opening I beheld some of the lovely things the sky contains; thence we came out, and saw again the stars," Dante, *Inferno*, 397.—Trans.

Chapter 8

The Primacy of Wisdom

SPIRITUALITY BASED ON WISDOM is not monolithic and exclusivist. Wisdom does not shut the horizons of the spirit, but it expands them to the extent in which it raises the vision of the world and of life to the supreme summit of all things, God. Above all, this spirituality governs the relationship between man and God.

All the natural and supernatural faculties (i.e., the virtues corresponding to human faculties and tendencies) are thus strengthened, stimulated, and decidedly directed towards the worship of God in contemplation and action.

On the real basis of human nature, the intellect and will that seek their own good are developed in the intellectual and moral virtues. These virtues shape character and make the personality mature in an internal and external ordering in which man is docile to conscience, to reason, letting himself be guided in his conduct. But a new plant of grace is grafted in human nature, as participation of the divine nature, which blooms in faith, hope, and charity (corresponding to the faculty of intellect and will, to the capacity for knowledge and love). This new plant of grace also blooms in the infused moral virtues, which raise the virtuous human acts as to a superior octave. The infused moral virtues raise them to a supernatural sphere where the same forces and natural tendencies unfold in an activity that realizes divine values.

But the Holy Spirit works according to the laws of a proper economy above the rational principle and even the supra—rational principle that moves the soul in the economy of the virtues. The Holy Spirit makes the soul docile and easily moved and infuses it with the momentum, the impulse, the genius, and the originality that characterizes the new Christian personality in its most perfect expressions. The gifts of the Holy Spirit are but the dispositions and qualities of the soul to the action of this superior principle, as the virtues are by relation to the dictates and the impulse of human reason. That notion of an arcane force that in a superior way operates in the genius and in the hero, which the pagans already formulated (as Aristotle did in the chapter "*De bona fortuna*" of his *Eudemian Ethics*),[1] becomes a reality in the Christian soul where the Holy Spirit operates and infuses his gifts.

Among the gifts, and therefore among all the virtues which the gifts perfect, primacy belongs to wisdom.[2]

In fact, wisdom is a refinement of faith which, as adherence to the truth of God living in Christ, is a participation of the eternal wisdom that binds the divine persons in a communion of light, so that the life of faith is a participation in the Trinitarian circuit of knowledge and of love in which the true divinization of man is realized.

But in this earthly stage of the supernatural life, participation in the Trinitarian light is always imperfect and full of uncertainties, obscurity, and doubts, so that union with God often appears to us as an arduous good and far away. However, hope intervenes. It is infused by God, and, as a virtue, transfers the foundation of our expectation and desires so that they are founded in God whom alone we come to seek as the true and total Good to be attained. Hope represents in the soul a participation of the eternal impetus with which the divine Persons attract and possess themselves in the unity of divinity. The Holy Spirit himself is this divine, attractive, unifying and expansive impulse.

---

1. Aristotle, *Eudemian Ethics*, VIII, 1247a, 1–14; 1248 a, 14–29. See Rackham, *Eudemian*, 454–56 and 464–66. —Trans.

2. Cf. *ST*, I–II, q. 68, a. 3–8; *ST*, II–II, q. 8, a. 6; *ST*, II–II q. 9, a. 2, etc.

In making himself present as a guest of the soul, the Holy Spirit is also communicated to the soul as charity, as a mysterious possession of the beloved God, because God is good in itself. In him, the soul pours itself out almost coming out of itself, dying to self, to be in the beloved and with the beloved. As gift of uncreated love, the Holy Spirit awakens in the soul reverence, aspiration, and possession.

Wisdom completes these virtues, like the flower of the whole supernatural plant, and makes them perform its acts in an exquisite way, impregnating them with a divine aroma.

In this new climate, the infused moral virtues raise the whole moral life and all practical conduct to the level of "new creation," of the "new man" that grace and the theological virtues form and nourish. The infused moral virtues do this without eliminating either the natural faculty or the virtues that develop in them by their own strength through their exercise. Given the tendency for grace to harmony of nature, the human way of living, acting, and thinking is perfected according to the dictates of reason enlightened and refined by faith and under the impulse of the will moved and rectified by the Spirit. It is the regimen of prudence.

But the gifts of the Holy Spirit intervene to give the soul a divine way of acting, in the same fields of virtues that are perfected, but they do it according to a judgment and a motion that man accepts from God with complete docility, well beyond his human judgments and designs. Thus the understanding makes one perceive the profound sense of revealed truth, and knowledge helps to distinguish it with exactness from error. Both do this while perfecting faith. But wisdom brings to the heights the capacity of faith to consider everything in the light of God; and in this light, it develops the moral life, where council perfects prudence, Christian fortitude human courage, piety the religious sense that flourishes from justice, and the fear of God perfects temperance.[3]

3. Cf. *ST*, II–II, q. 8, a. 6; q. 9, a. 2; q. 45, ad 1, 2.

Chapter 9

The Sins against Wisdom

To THE ONE WHO becomes his servant, wisdom gives a beatitude and spiritual height, which is a splendid aspect of the royalty of the servants of God. To serve God is to reign. St. Paul says: "all belong to you, and you to Christ, and Christ to God" (1 Cor 3:22–23).

But one can fail wisdom with specific sins, which turns into the worst spiritual disaster. Then it becomes the failure of life according to wisdom, and this means the dissolution of a whole system of spirituality.

Above all, the failure is a matter of spiritual blindness, caecitas mentis, or the privation of the "intelligible principle" of inner vision.[1]

This intelligible principle is threefold: first, reason itself as the natural faculty of knowledge, which can be lost through a mental illness; second, the light of faith and grace, of which one can be deprived, partially in this life and fully and definitively in the afterlife (hell), as punishment for sin; and third, the first truth itself, the living truth, which is God. In God, wisdom is to know, love, and enjoy the supreme things, the most unfathomable mysteries. But a soul can depart from God either because it directly and formally rejects him, as in the case of a real atheism and impiety, or because it allows itself to be distracted and attracted by things that enchant it in opposition to God, as in the case of

1. Cf. *ST*, II–II, q. 15, a. 1.

THE SINS AGAINST WISDOM

worldliness, dissipation, sensuality, and frivolity. These attitudes
of rejection or distraction easily lead to the "blindness of the
mind." It leads to the state of those who, for lack of that light, are
deprived of "any knowledge of spiritual goods."[2] It is a sin against
the gift of understanding. The gift of understanding allows the
pure of heart to "see God." It allows the pure of heart to have a
deep, acute, and very fine perception. By diminishing God on the
horizon of the mind, the ability to read inwardly and deeply the
heights and depths of things he has written in the universe, in the
gospel, and in the human spirit is diminished. This explains so
many phenomena of inner darkness, of blindness before the sun
of the spirit, which daily experience shows.

Sin against the spirit of wisdom also takes on another aspect:
that of dullness of sense. The latter is a certain obtuseness that an-
tagonizes the mental acuity of the one who possesses the "principle of intelligibility." The spiritual sense, in similarity to the bodily
senses, has the ability to penetrate, to intuit, and to experience
spiritual things with readiness and agility. If one loses it, however,
one becomes spirituality stupid and obtuse. One becomes "weak-
minded in the consideration of spiritual goods,"[3] and is always in
opposition to the gift of understanding which gave that capacity
for penetration and growth. Then annoyance arises and therefore
negligence for spiritual things, which is already a sin.[4]

In a more direct contrast to wisdom, one can have foolishness,[5]
which is a sort of stupor of the mind and of the heart joined to the
obtuseness of feeling, as a result of which one becomes incapable
of judgment, discernment, or a sense of responsibility.

The wise one has the sense or faculty of judgment and is
subtle and perspicacious; the fool has it blunted; the fatuous has
lost it completely.[6]

2. *ST*, II–II, q. 15, a. 2.
3. *ST*, II–II, q. 15, a. 2.
4. *ST*, II–II, q. 15, a. 2.
5. *ST*, II–II, q. 46, a. 1.
6. *ST*, II–II, q. 46, a. 1.

Needless to say, it is a matter of the state of the soul in its relationship with God in the spiritual life. Foolishness is an obtuseness of the spirit by which nothing is understood about God any more. One does not perceive his transcendent evidence; one cannot judge things in his light, namely, "by the highest causes." It is the situation of the *animalis homo*, to be precise, of man linked to his nature in his earthly heaviness and closed to the spirit of God. Such a man does not accept what pertains to the Spirit of God (1 Cor 2:14). He is "as man whose taste is infected by an evil humor and sweet things have no savor for [him]."[7]

Perhaps nobody wants to arrive at this foolishness. But such foolishness is the logical consequence, or the other side, of any excessive abandonment to earthly things and to any unruly sensual delight, especially in the field of lust.[8] Also, this foolishness is the consequence of any departure from the contemplation of truth, which is a precept of God's law.[9]

The cause of this foolishness is especially in the abuse of the senses that occurs in the sins of the flesh, namely gluttony and lust.[10] Gluttony and lust plunge a person so deep into the domain of materiality as to prevent the mind from detaching itself from the world of sensitive images to rise to the summits of divine truth, which one can glimpse with the gift of understanding. The action of the gift of understanding is frustrated by lust. Lust produces blindness of mind, while gluttony renders you spiritually stupid and obtuse. The consequence of all this is foolishness and the loss of wisdom, because wisdom cannot have a place in a soul absorbed by earthly pleasures.[11]

The cultivation of wisdom, if it is sincere, implies the mortification of the senses with the practice of the "virtues opposed to gluttony and lust. A sincere cultivation of wisdom implies the practice of abstinence and chastity, which most of all dispose man to

7. *ST,* II–II, q. 46, a. 2.
8. *ST,* II–II, q. 46, a. 2, ad 2.
9. *ST,* II–II, q. 46, a.2, ad 3.
10. *ST,* II–II, q. 15, a. 3.
11. *ST,* II–II, q. 46, a. 3.

the perfection of intellectual activity."[12] These virtues dispose man to contemplation and to the exercise of wisdom.

The whole tradition of Christian spirituality includes and develops the notion of mortification as much as possible. There is no saint who has not practiced it, sometimes reaching extreme points which are not normally imitable. In founding an apostolic order, St. Dominic also wanted to insert in his organic constitution the penitential element, along with the liturgical element that had been affirmed above all in the canonical life. The penitential element was expressed especially in monastic life. One and the other are ordered to contemplation and to the apostolate.

Thus, in sapiential spirituality, it is not only study as an intense and constant use of natural faculties that counts. It is not just brains you need. This intellectual power can be abundant and strong even in the worldly and can coexist with carnal sins; but, in such cases, it does not serve much for contemplation, from which those sins distract.[13]

Study requires, as penitential practice, a discipline of intelligence that is a means of preparation for contemplation and for the apostolate. And along with it, study requires the other penitential practices and observances which lead to "purity of heart." Abstinence and silence especially enable the soul to live in an enclosure of internal and external peace and in an atmosphere of silence and solitude, where the soul can remain in dialogue with God.

The moral virtues create the dispositions to purity and order in the sensitive part of the soul. The gift of understanding completes the work, freeing the mind from the tyranny of sensible imaginations and making it penetrate into the pure intelligible,[14] where wisdom makes the soul taste the mystery of God.

12. *ST,* II–II, q. 15, a. 3.
13. *ST,* II–II, q. 15, a. 3, ad 1.
14. *ST,* II–II, q. 8, a. 7.

Chapter 10

Wisdom in Religious Life

AGAINST THE DANGERS OF foolishness and in order to reach wisdom safely, Jesus has shown to those who wish to follow him the path of total consecration to him and to his kingdom with the evangelical counsels. These are voluntary poverty, perfect chastity, and self-denial, which are especially accomplished in obedience to a superior. These counsels have been embraced and practiced from the beginning in Christian communities, and they gradually became the basic points of schools and institutions of spiritual life, up to the establishment of the "religious orders." In these institutions, the counsels are embraced with vows, which are exquisitely religious acts recognized and approved by the Church.

Religious life is therefore a state of perfection in which man consecrates himself by means of vows in service to God.

There are different types of religious orders. Some, the most ancient ones and the most perfect as regards their essential element, are religious orders of contemplative life. In them, the service to God is realized and manifested above all by contemplation and by the elevation of the mind to God. In these religious orders, it is the gift of wisdom which has its full expansion. They are religious orders of the worship of wisdom. They have a stable official worship, institutionalized in them as social groupings, but which must reproduce itself in the contemplative life of their members.

The contemplative life is proper to those whose main task is the contemplation of the truth. As St. Thomas says, it is proper to those "who are chiefly intent on the contemplation of truth."[1] Contemplation is an activity of the intellect, but it has roots in the will, in the heart, because the intention that leads to contemplation is an act of the will. The will in its acts is moved by an object that elicits its essential act, namely love. The act of tendency to contemplation of God is therefore the love of God, which, according to the very psychology of love, is resolved in an ardent desire to know, contemplate, and taste the object of love, namely the eternal truth and beauty ("Since through loving God we are aflame to gaze on His beauty."[2]).

Like its beginning, so the end of contemplation is love, because the knowledge of truth as "lovable good" fills the soul with affection and delight.[3] To study, to know God, to live in dialogue and communion with him, and to go up to him on the way of wisdom responds to the yearning of charity towards the vision of the "first Principle" in the search for God, which is so connatural to man.[4]

That there are religious orders in which this contemplative activity takes places exclusively, or primarily, is a great resource for souls thirsting for wisdom. It is also a great resource for the Church, which receives the benefit of exemplars, of the testimony to the "one thing necessary," of the fruits of prayer and penance of their members.

Now, there can be a synthesis of contemplation and action in the religious orders instituted for preaching and teaching others. This synthesis is meant to give spiritual goods as an expansion of contemplation itself,[5] or even just to study. In fact, study is of help to contemplation, because it illuminates the intellect and preserves it from errors, which are always a danger to contemplatives. Study is necessary for those who must preach and

1. *ST,* II–II, q. 180, a. 1.
2. *ST,* II–II, q. 180, a. 1.
3. *ST,* II–II, q. 180, a. 1, ad 1.
4. *ST,* II–II, q. 180, a.1, ad 2.
5. *ST,* II–II, q. 180, a. 4.

teach. Study is useful as an ascetic exercise to avoid temptations, especially lust.[6] It is, therefore, a more than sufficient reason to justify a religious order, as a way of wisdom.

Among the religious orders, those of contemplative life surpass those of active life, as we have said. However, even when a religious order has as its task the works of spiritual and apostolic active life, such as preaching and teaching ("go and teach" . . .); it reaches the summit of institutional perfection, because such works are born from the fullness of contemplation. And the lives of those who dedicate themselves to it are not only shining but also illuminating, giving others the light of the contemplated truth. "Even as it is better to enlighten than merely to shine, so it is better to give to others the fruits of one's contemplation than merely to contemplate."[7]

For the fulfillment of this task, the common life is normally necessary, except for periodic breaks in solitude, which is good "for a time" to restore strength, to collect oneself more quietly in God, and to carefully make a review of one's life.[8]

The community serves, can and must serve, as an aid both to the intellect by instruction and education to contemplation and to the will, the heart. The community instructs the heart with the fellowship and solidarity that it offers by example and witness of a holy life that it puts before the eyes of its members. The witness of a holy life, which it facilitates among its various members, is offered with reciprocal correction of defects and shortcomings. Hence with these forms of collaboration, it helps the path of every soul on the way to wisdom.

But it is the gift of wisdom that presides over all this personal and communitarian religious activity. It is the gift of wisdom that makes us seek the truth ("a wise man will seek the truth" . . .) and urges us to communicate it ("without envy I share" . . .), as

---

6. *ST,* II–II, q. 188, a. 5.

7. *ST,* II–II, q. 188, a. 6: "*Sicut enim maius est illuminare quam lucere solum, ita maius est contemplata aliis tradere quam solum contemplari.*"

8. *ST,* II–II, q. 188, a. 8.

it happened for St. Thomas Aquinas.[9] It is the gift of wisdom that causes the soul to unite so much with God and to speak only *of* him or about him, as was said of St. Dominic by witnesses to the process of his canonization. It is the gift of wisdom that, even in the scientific preparation for contemplation through study, makes it possible not to become pure scholars, pure intellectuals, arid cerebrals, but lovers of Truth, that is, lovers of God. It is the gift of wisdom that not only on the summits of mystical contemplation but also in theology, in philosophy, and it can be said in every discipline, makes lovers of the eternal Wisdom. Eternal Wisdom is the only true wisdom which is also life.

This is the fundamental meaning of Dominican religious life.

9. *SG*, 1, I, c. 2.

Chapter 11

Religious Vows as Paths of Wisdom

THE OBSTACLES ON THE path of wisdom are primarily those listed by St. John as attitudes of the soul in opposition to the kingdom of God: "sensual lust, enticement for the eyes, and a pretentious life" (1 John 2:16). All Christian life is an ascetic exercise; for it takes a militia to fight these enemies of the soul and these dangers to the kingdom of God.

The most radical and heroic form of combat is that of religious vows. These types of vows are the maximum expansion of the baptismal ones, which in their ascetic aspect are a total renunciation not only of the sins that result from carnal and spiritual concupiscence (as by all Christians in baptism), but also a renunciation of events, roles, and possessions that are in themselves good. These goods can easily become occasions of deviance or excess. Therefore, these goods can become occasions of sin, of spiritual folly, and of estrangement from the way of wisdom.

Now, in their religious aspect, the vows mark the total consecration of the soul in the service of God. But they do not constitute the essence of perfection. The essence of perfection consists in charity,[1] from which the way of wisdom begins and ends again in the fullness of love. The vows are instead a means of charity and paths of wisdom. Together, however, the vows reveal that in

---

1. *ST*, II–II, q. 186, a. 1.

the soul that professes them, love is abundant, and the desire for wisdom is great.

The interpretation that, on this basis, St. Thomas Aquinas gives of the vows is crystal clear.

The vow of poverty responds to Jesus's counsel to "sell" or "leave" everything to follow him (Matt 19:21; Mark 10:21; Luke 18:22). In order to achieve total affective liberation from slavery to worldly things, "it is necessary that a man wholly withdraw his affections from worldly things,"[2] and that he becomes a servant of true wisdom. The vow of poverty is the overcoming of psychological alienation established by the attachment to the goods of the earth by cupidity, by avarice, and by the idolatry of money and comfort. St. Thomas argues that especially wealth "does not conduce to the happiness of the contemplative life, rather it is an obstacle thereto, inasmuch as the anxiety it involves disturbs the quiet of the soul."[3]

Whoever wants to dedicate himself to the worship of wisdom needs this peace and spiritual freedom. He needs this agility of soul that, on the basis of a sufficient security guaranteed by the common life, finds in "religious life" the space to train on the path of perfection. Above all, whoever in a more formal, conscious, and intense way feels called and wants to live in the spirituality characterized by the worship of wisdom, finds in poverty the first path to the ideal that attracts him.

The second path is that of perfect chastity. This is a vow that aims at removing those other obstacles which, standing on the way of perfect service to God and the worship of wisdom, are created by the pleasures of the flesh and by the cares of the family and domestic life.[4] One and the other do not imply an intrinsic reason of moral evil. They are good things in themselves and must represent, for those called to live in the secular world, the constant exercise of the virtue of temperance. Temperance is not insensitivity and

2. *ST*, II–II, q. 186, a. 3: "*ut aliquis totaliter abstrahat affectum suum a rebus mundanis . . . .*"

3. *ST*, II–II, q. 186, a. 3, ad 4.

4. *ST*, II–II, q. 186, a. 4.

rejection of the joy of life, or rejection of the pleasure attached to licit sexual relations within marriage, or rejection of the use of all the senses. The joy of life and legitimate pleasures also represent the constant exercise of charity. They also represent the exercise of the other social virtues within the family and on the wider area of human community, where each one is called to commit himself to cooperate in the common good.

But he who feels called and intends to devote himself more freely to the things of God can respond to his vocation by renouncing even pleasures such as marriage and family, which in themselves are positive values. And he can, through consecration of his own body to God, become fruitful in a different way. He thus conquers and exercises a more profound freedom, as St. Thomas says when speaking of virginity, and moves towards a progressive elevation of the spirit in the contemplation of divine truth (so that there is more freedom to give oneself to the contemplation of truth).[5]

Obedience is the vow that responds to the invitation of Jesus to deny oneself and to follow him even to the point of denying one's own independence and to give him one's faculty of decision and autonomous movement. This vow also responds to the call to accept the authority of a superior, as an image of and in place of the divine master. In the Thomist and Dominican model in particular, the superior is considered as one of the teachers of spirituality and of the common life.[6] He is called to act prudently and charitably within the boundaries of the legitimate and reasonable exercise of his office. His directives exert a binding force on the will of those who have freely elected him. Another way of looking at it is from the point of view of those who live religious life under a superior. They know the superior has been given a specific mission to guard,

5. *ST,* II–II, q. 152, a.2.

6. Citing the Rule of St. Augustine, the current Dominican Constitutions (no. 20 § III) state the following about the superior: "Seeking God's will and the good of the community, the superior should regard himself to be fortunate as one who serves you in love, not as one who exercises authority over you. He ought to foster willing service rather than slavish submission." *Constitutions,* 50.—Trans.

defend, and apply as the successor and representative of the holy Founder, and indeed, of Christ, the sole Teacher and Master (Matt 23:8). They also know the superior cannot command them to do anything that is contrary to reason, to God's revelation and law, to their own Constitutions, or the teachings of the Church.

In this light, religious obedience reveals its dignity and also appears as an overcoming of the innermost alienation of the ego, which sometimes can easily become a slave to itself, to its own preferences, and to its own narrow and wrong views, and to its own worst inclinations. The vow of obedience thus works out an achievement of inner freedom.

The vow of obedience implies a sincere and intelligent external and internal deference to the "teacher" who represents the "Teacher." It is deference without antagonisms and without conformism, but with manly and humble self–offering. A self–offering that is consistent with the renunciation and consecration that the vow brings even to the root of all human activity: the will.

Obedience is a *necessity* to which the will has committed itself and continually commits itself with free decision and self–offering, generating perfection, wisdom, and merit. As St. Thomas writes:

> The necessity which is consequent upon obedience is a necessity not of coercion (*necessitas coactionis*) but of free will, inasmuch as a man is willing to obey, although perhaps he would not be willing to do the thing commanded considered in itself. Wherefore, since by the vow of obedience a man lays himself under the necessity of doing for God's sake certain things that are not pleasing in themselves, for this very reason that which he does is the more acceptable to God, though it be of less account, because a man can give nothing greater to God, than by subjecting his will to another man's for God's sake.[7]

This is why obedience is the highest and most fundamental vow in which other vows are also included.[8]

---

7. *ST,* II–II, q. 186, a. 5, ad 5.
8. *ST,* II–II, q. 186, a. 8.

The wisdom of the world shrinks from these vows and now perhaps especially from obedience. In contrast, the wisdom that God gives as a gift of the Spirit prompts us along these paths towards the perfection of love.

Chapter 12

Wisdom and Prayer

THE CONTEMPLATIVE ACT, WHICH has its root in wisdom, flourishes in prayer. Prayer is the elevation of the soul to God in a discourse made up of notions and feelings which sometimes express themselves in words, and sometimes vibrate in silence. Both the word and the silence in prayer carry within themselves a charge of wisdom that contemplates, admires, loves, adores, relishes, and sings.

Devotion is born of contemplative wisdom, because this reveals the goodness of God to the soul and makes it understand the limit and defects of human capacities and faculties.[1] The voice that invokes help and mercy rises from the experience of limitations when confronted with knowledge of the infinite.

It is a process lived by the contemplative and prayerful soul. A process that, for Christians, takes place through the mediation of Christ, whose humanity, studied and contemplated, inspires devotion in the soul to guide it and make it concentrate on God.[2]

Reaching God in light, the soul is taken by the joy of infinite truth; and, at the same time, the soul experiences a sense of sadness before its own limitations and misery.[3] Rejoicing and suffering are the steady rhythm in the psychology of a piety that contemplates

1. *ST*, II–II, q. 82, a. 3.
2. *ST*, II–II, q. 82, a.3 ad 2.
3. *ST*, II–II, q. 82, a. 4.

and prays. Concerning feelings and affections, the will and the passions are projected into the spiritual life with the human charge, which finds expression in concepts and words above all of pain and of joy. In both cases, it is a work of love.

The contemplative act is essentially in the intellect, where the ascent of the mind to God is carried out. This is proper of the rational creature,[4] but it arises under the impulse of the will and of love.[5] And therefore, it is easily translated into devotion and into prayer. It does not remain in the world of ideas. It does not take shape only in forms of mental abstraction, but seeks affections and words to become a loving dialogue with God.

This is prayer. It is born in every soul when it rises to God yielding to its attraction. It is made of intimate words, which sometimes take a voice, becoming even external words (*vocal prayer*), both because these excite more internal devotion, and also because the voice, in its physicality, must pay tribute to God. Above all, it is so by a redundancy of the soul which in its affective fullness also involves the whole world of sentiments and of human words in order to open up and rise up to God in the totality of man.[6] When prayer becomes common, it is almost necessarily vocal, because the voice offers those who pray together the possibility of forming a choir and feeling it.

But what matters most is that prayer be attentive, more according to the spirit than according to the letter of the words. It also needs to be attentive according to the letter, as far as possible, because the relationship with God cannot but be conscious absorbed concentration and demanding that the mind be in discourse with him. It must also be lasting, continuous, as it is in the psychology of charity which, being love, leads to prolonged discourses with the beloved. Although when it is prolonged, it is then necessary to contain prayer in a framework of compatibility both with others and with the general and particular state of those

4. *ST*, II–II, q. 83, a. 1.
5. *ST*, II–II, q. 83, a. 1, ad 1, 2.
6. *ST*, II–II, q. 83, a. 12.

who pray. Therefore, one can also fix a certain program of times, places, and ways of prayer.

In our time, it seems that, to some, prayer is not suitable for a humanity that has become used to thinking great powerful self-sufficient thoughts, and, on its own, is able to free itself from all alienations and slavery. In contrast, prayer is born of the recognition of the Other, of God, as infinite and holy and of the experience of our own need and our own nothingness. Prayer is the voice of poverty.

But even in the heart of a civilization of technology and positive science, there is no man who at a certain moments does not feel the need and the longing for totality, for perfection, and for the infinite. Even if all the calamities and sufferings of the world were overcome, the problem of the soul remains open. The human person still needs the eternal, the infinite. It is not possible to always silence this need, or to falsify its voice. The cry of the heart will sooner or later rise, even as voices over the abyss.

Wisdom can teach and inspire suitable prayer for the man of today.

Yes, wisdom can inspire a prayer of petition, a request, but not for particular graces (though this is not to be excluded or neglected). What's more, prayer is not simply a request for "miracles" (especially healings, good business results, etc.). But wisdom can inspire a prayer for all being, for having, doing, loving, thinking, etc., for all the dynamism of "secondary causes" and for all existential and vital development. This is so, because wisdom makes us know and feel that everything comes from God. All is God's, and it returns to God, beginning and end, source and channel, alpha and omega of the universe. God is all of this especially for the human self, for its life story, for love and pain, its realization of sociability and communion with others. Prayer is a petition that also becomes thanksgiving, because you ask for what you already have and are receiving ever anew.

It is also a prayer of praise, adoration, and contemplation, which expresses the admiration that in today's man can be more abundant and frequent than it was in the man of yesterday, precisely because in the civilization of the positive sciences and technology, the inerrable wonders created by God are better brought to light. There will be more or less long pauses, or perhaps no exclusively contemplative pause (but it would be an evil for today's man), before these wonders, but it will be above all an experience, a welcome, a participation, and therefore a feeling caught in the soul by amazement and then by the need of an ever-new *Benedicite*.

The prayer of benediction seems the most congenial to today's man. It can translate into praise expressed with word and with song.[7] In this case, heart and mouth, soul and body are united in the celebration of God, personally and collectively. What matters most, however, will always be the praise of the heart, without which the mouth says and does useless things. "It profits nothing to praise with the lips if one praise not with the heart."[8] Indeed, no aestheticism must prevail in prayer, in singing, or in sacred music, because it would inspire more of a taste for earthly things, or even spiritual delight, than true religious devotion.[9] However, especially in collective celebrations, the poetic, musical, and allegorical praise of God has an efficacious and elevating effect on the souls that help each other in devotion and worship.[10] For even sacred art is part of the economy of *laus Deus*, as well as that of the pedagogy of faith and piety. Hence we see the importance of liturgy even as a school of piety.

But it is especially in the depth of souls that the source of prayer is to be sought. The gift of wisdom acts as a herald of light. The gift of piety acts as a herald of filial affection for the God whom we contemplate. Filial affection translates into invoking him as a father.[11] It is the Spirit that makes us adoptive sons of God, who makes us call him father (Rom 8:26) as by a mysterious instinct that acts in the depths and impels us towards him with the gift of piety. ("By this gift, we offer service and honor to God

7. *ST*, II–II, q. 91, a. 1.
8. *ST*, II–II, q. 91, a. 1, ad 2.
9. *ST*, II–II, q. 91, a. 1, ad 3; a. 2 ad 2–5.
10. *ST*, II–II, q. 91, a. 2.
11. *ST*, II–II, q. 121, a. 1.

as our father under the prompting of the Holy Spirit"). Piety is a gift by which we manifest our service and duty to God as father by an instinct of the Holy Spirit. Piety is also a gift by which we manifest our duty to our fellow man as brothers, inasmuch as they are sons of God just as we are.[12]

Thus piety translates into worship, into prayer, and in homage to the heavenly Father. It translates into the sentiments and contemplations which are the fruit of wisdom, and into the "spirit of adoption" by which wisdom reaches the beatitude of the children of God.

Thus the sapiential prayer is tender, intense, and pleasant like the contemplation it inspires. St. Dominic, St. Thomas, and St. Catherine prayed this way.

12. *ST,* II–II, q. 121, a. 1, ad 3.

Chapter 13

Wisdom and the Sacraments

LIFE ACCORDING TO WISDOM is inaugurated and developed in the soul through the gifts of the Holy Spirit. These gifts descend from on high and operate from the depths as dispositions and energies through which God takes on and exercises the full government of human life.

Man receives these gifts. By them, he is raised to a sphere of life that is well beyond the ordinary trajectory of human spirituality. That is to say, he is raised to asceticism, which is an effort to conquer in order to implement self-mastery. He is raised to prayer, which is the invocation of divine aid; and he is raised to mysticism itself, which is contemplation and conscious possession of God. Beyond this summit, contemplation, prayer, and the enjoyment of God are prolonged and accentuated to the extent that the gifts are multiplied in spiritual richness by ever new interventions of God in the soul.

This donative and creative intervention takes place especially in the sacraments, where God is met and gives grace to all those who seek him. The sacraments mark the stages of God who comes and the soul that goes into him. They mark the stages of life according to wisdom, which develops in the Christian in imitation of that of Jesus, who as a boy and as a young man, "grew in wisdom before God and men" (Luke 1:80).

Baptism is a birth into the new life, which the ancient tradition of the Church and the Fathers called "illuminatio." According to St. Thomas, this sacrament gives the members of the Body of Christ (*Corpus Christi*) the life of light, because,

> Again, just as the members derive sense and movement from the material head, so from the spiritual head, i.e. Christ, do His members derive spiritual sense consisting in the knowledge of truth, and spiritual movement which results from the instinct of grace . . . And it follows from this that the baptized are enlightened by Christ as to the knowledge of the truth, and made fruitful by Him with the fruitfulness of good works by the infusion of grace.[1]

Baptism is therefore an illumination of the soul, a true birth in light. The "salt of wisdom," which is administered by baptism, is like the symbol of the new life of the spirit granted to the soul.

Confirmation is a strengthening of the soul with the gifts of the Spirit, which make it capable of witnessing to the divine richness before others and of enlightening them with the light of wisdom realized inwardly. The apostolate as enlightenment of all on the dimensions of Christ's wisdom and charity (Eph 3:8, 18–19; Col 2:3) has in this sacrament its divine—ecclesial root.[2]

Penance is the sacrament of the return to wisdom. Specifically, it is the return to purity of heart and to the freedom of the children of God.[3]

The Eucharist is the feast of wisdom, far richer, more effective, and vital than the Platonic symposium and the Dantean banquet, because in it is present eternal Wisdom itself, Christ. He is the

---

1. *ST*, III, q. 69, a. 5. cf *ST*, III, q. 69, ad 2: on the relationship between external illumination ("the teacher enlightens outwardly and ministerially by catechizing") and interior illumination ("but God enlightens the baptized inwardly, by preparing their hearts for the reception of the doctrines of truth"), St. Thomas appeals to the Gospel text: "They shall all be taught by God" (John 6:45; cf. Isa 54:13).

2. Cf. *ST*, III, q. 72, a. 2, ad 1: "the Apostles were filled with the Holy Ghost, as teachers of the faith; but the rest of the believers, as doing that which gives edification to the faithful. . . . " And *ST*, III, q. 72, a. 2, ad 2, 3; a. 5, ad 2.

3. Cf. *ST*, III, q. 86, a. 5, sed contra; *ST*, III, q. 89, a. 3.

living bread descended from heaven (John 6:33–35), which is given as food to the soul under the sensible species of bread and wine. As St. Thomas says in the office of Corpus Christi: "Wisdom has built her house ... mixed her wine, yes, she has spread her table" (Prov 9:1–2).[4] It is the living wisdom that invites us to the banquet where we eat him, where the *"panis angelicus"* become *"panis hominum"* in a celebration where the contemplation of the mystery so easily translates into praise, poetry, and singing:

Adoro te devote, latens Deitas ...

Lauda, Sion, Salvatorem,
lauda Ducem et Pastorem
in hymnis et canticis.

Pange, lingua, gloriosi
Corporis mysterium
Sanguinisque pretiosi
quem in mundi pretium,
fructum ventris generosi
Rex effudit gentium ...[5]

Sublime synthesis of theology and of mystical contemplation and poetry!

The anointing of the sick is the last preparation for eternal contemplation, which in heaven is the vision of God. It is the sacrament of the passage from shadowy wisdom to the most luminous wisdom of celestial glory. It is the last and the definitive infusion

---

4. I *Antiph. In Laudibus.* Here the author is referring to the antiphon before the reading from Scripture of the Office of Readings for the Feast of Corpus Christi in the Liturgy of the Hours. See *Liturgia*, 533.—Trans. See also *ST*, III, q. 79, a. 1, 2, and 6; q. 80, a. 1; q. 82, a. 3, ad 3, etc.

5. According to Britt, the first line (*Adoro te devote*) is from a hymn in honor of the Eucharist written by St. Thomas Aquinas. Britt, *Hymns*, 190. Fr. Spiazzi does not cite sources for the other full stanzas, which are not from the same hymn but from two different hymns for the feast of *Corpus Christi*: the *Lauda Sion Salvatorem* and the *Pange Lingua.* Britt, *Hymns*, 178 and 183.—Trans.

of Christian wisdom that since baptism has operated in the soul to realize the right ordering of the whole life to God.[6]

The sacrament of holy orders makes and consecrates the ministers of wisdom and the administrators of the people of God. The bishops are consecrated as teachers of divine truth and hierarchical guides of life according to wisdom. The priests and other ministers are consecrated as collaborators of the bishops in the ordering and governance of the Church according to wisdom. In other words, they collaborate in the ordering and governing according to a supernatural vision and a perspective of eternity.[7] This is the true secret of the priestly apostolate.

Marriage, as a sacrament, is a work of love enlightened by Christian wisdom which makes one discover and contemplate in it the reproduction of the nuptial mystery of Christ and the Church (Eph 5:32).[8] Marriage guides and comforts the spouses in the fulfillment of their mission, which is of procreation, education, and support of those children of man and children of God. In the Christian family, these children can and must grow in the likeness of Jesus, "in age and in wisdom" (Luke 2:52), until they reach, with the help of their parents, "the perfect age," the "stature" of Christ (Eph 4:13) in whom they are predestined.

Thus the spiritual life is for everyone, in all states of life, a work of wisdom that comes from above (Jas 3:17), as a continuous and ever new gift from the heavenly Father. The sacraments are its vehicle. Above all, the Christian, the religious soul, can and must count on them to reach on the way of wisdom, the ultimate end of their vocation.

6. Cf. *ST*, Suppl., III P., q. 30, a. 1.

7. Cf. *ST*, Suppl. III P., q. 34, a. 1; q. 37, a. 1 and a. 2; q. 40, a. 6.

8. Cf. *ST*, Suppl. III P., q. 42, a. 2.

Chapter 14

The Seat of Wisdom

THE LITURGY ATTRIBUTES TO Mary many things that the holy scriptures say of eternal wisdom, the Word of God who assumed human nature in the bosom of the young woman of Nazareth, making her his throne, his seat. Therefore, Mary is invoked as the seat of wisdom in this ontological sense, which tells of the link between the Mother and the Son in eternal predestination and in the historical realization of the mystery of the redemptive incarnation. Even from the psychological point of view, Mary is Seat of Wisdom (*Sedes Sapientiae*), because her spirit, no less than her bosom, has opened itself to divine wisdom, and by receiving it in herself, she has taken possession of it, and has become a tabernacle.

The Magnificat is a canticle that expresses what the soul of Mary has intimately realized about the discovery, awareness, experience, and revelation of God. It is a song of praise and thanksgiving. At the same time, it is a song of proclamation, of exaltation of God before Elizabeth, before the first Christian communities, and before all those who, throughout the centuries, wish to welcome him. The Magnificat is a proclamation that says God has worked the mercy promised to his people. Thus the interior vision becomes song, and the sapiential contemplation is poured out in the apostolate. Action flows from contemplation. To give to others the things contemplated.[1]

1. *ST*, II–II, q. 188, a. 6; *ST*, III, q. 40, a. 1, ad 2.

Therefore, all those who live in the service of wisdom can look to Mary as Seat of Wisdom (*Sedes Sapientiae*) and honor her above all with the rosary. Praying the rosary makes them contemplate, in the "mysteries," the "mystery of the Kingdom of God" actualized in Mary. This mystery came about in Mary by her perfect participation in the mystery of Christ, to whom the Christian soul conforms according to the wisdom of the gospel.

"Our Lady of the Rosary" and "*Sedes Sapientiae*" are Marian titles that substantially coincide. Both make us recognize and invoke Mary, because she is, in a special way, at the center of the economy of salvation which is object of contemplation and of the apostolate.

Not without a profound reason have the Dominicans cultivated and propagated devotion to Mary as Queen of the Holy Rosary. One of their most beautiful and best known churches in Rome is Santa Maria sopra Minerva, which was built over an ancient temple of the pagan goddess of wisdom. In Mary, they saw symbolically represented and historically realized the eternal ideal of contemplative wisdom. In Mary, they saw at work the "good news" of salvation, which is the raison d'être of their Order and the synthesis of their spirituality and of their apostolate.

An explicit and conscious devotion to Our Lady Seat of Wisdom can flourish from devotion to the rosary, as a veneration of Mary considered in relation to wisdom.

Mary is indeed the Mother of Divine Wisdom, which appeared in the world in human form. She is the mother of the Word made flesh, which under her eyes grew in wisdom (Luke 2:52) and "full of grace and truth" (John 1:14).

Mary is the first contemplative of the divine mysteries. She saw these divine mysteries developing in her son's life, and she reflected on them in her heart (Luke 2:19), as a rosary of life of which she was participant as well as spectator.

Mary is an apostle of wisdom in Hebron, where she sings the Magnificat; she is an apostle in Bethlehem, where she shows Jesus to the shepherds and to the wise men; in Nazareth, where she assimilates the mystery of the incarnation of the Word that she will then make known to the Church with the "Infancy Gospel"; in Jerusalem, where she presents him to the priests and to the prophetic souls of the Temple; at Cana, where she solicits his first miraculous manifestation; in Calvary, where he deepens the mystery of redemption, to which she will soon testify; in the Cenacle, where she supports the followers of Christ in prayer awaiting the Spirit; and in the primitive Christian community, where she provides news about the advent of Christ, including the truth of the incarnation.

Because of her special relationship with Jesus Christ, Mary is the mediator of wisdom, as well as mediator of every other grace that is granted to every man attracted by God to faith in Christ and to eternal salvation.

It is therefore a question of implementing a program of Marian and rosary devotion corresponding to the ideal of wisdom that we see concretized and realized in this woman who is "humbler and loftier than any creature, eternal counsel's predetermined goal."[2]

This means knowing her and studying her in the light in which God himself sees her, that is, associated with Christ at the center of the plan of salvation. She is certainly an historical figure, but full of mystery as an object of faith and of piety, and of contemplation. It means imitating her as a supreme example of union with God in contemplation, in prayer, and action. It means preaching about her and making her known as the greatest wonder of creation, after the humanity of Christ and in connection with it, especially for religious who, like the Dominicans, as affirmed by blessed Humbert of Romans, belong to an Order that is hers and was established principally to preach her truth and that of her son.[3]

The rosary serves this purpose. It is a school of contemplation for the sapiential knowledge of Christ and Mary. It is a synthesis of spirituality, which contains a treatise on Christian perfection as

2. Dante, *Paradiso*, 385.—Trans.

3. Humbert of Romans, *Expositio super Constitutiones*, 71. See Berthier, *Opera*, 71.—Trans. It is with great joy that we have seen this spirit of the Order confirmed, especially in reference to the rosary, in the new *Dominican Constitutions* (1968), nos. 67, 129.

it develops from contemplation and imitation of Christ with the help of Mary. The rosary is a practice of devotion entirely imbued with the spirit of wisdom which gives the soul knowledge and the enjoyment and the taste (*sapida scientia*) of divine things. Exercising and progressing in this pious practice is truly to walk on the path of perfection and to respond to the divine calling.

Chapter 15

The Bridegroom of Wisdom

DANTE ALIGHIERI SINGS OF Saint Dominic who:

> by his wisdom, was on earth,
> a splendor of Cherubic light.[1]

This is the rendition and poetic exaltation that Dante intuited about the fundamental value of the personality of St. Dominic: it was contemplative and enlightening wisdom and wisdom that expands into the apostolate.

It can also be said that St. Dominic is the spouse of Lady Wisdom, as St. Francis is of Lady Poverty.

There is a certain difference in mentality between the two saints, but also in the formulation of problems, in the style of life, and in their work, partly because their careers and their training are different.

Saint Francis is the jester of Assisi, who becomes the jester of God. He is the devoted knight that already suffers from the "dolce stil nuovo"[2] in the process of affirmation, and who, converted to

---

1. Dante, *Paradiso*, 123.—Trans.

2. This expression "the sweet new style" is found in Dante's *Purgatorio* Canto XXIV. According to Spiers, Dante claims Love as the inspiration for his poetry and by the use of this expression, "*dolce stil nuovo*," he associates himself with poets that had come before him and who used similar expressions. Spiers, "Vita," 38.—Trans.

Christ, brings back his poetic breath in terms of piety and religious witness in an exquisitely Italic tone.

Saint Dominic, his contemporary, is a Spanish knight and a descendant of a family of warriors trained in battles against the Moors. His character bears some air of this ancestry. But he is also a man of study, order, and prayer. He also knows, like St. Francis, the charismatic and prophetic impetus of the apostolate. But educated in strict studies and raised in a canonical Order, under an already fixed rule, St. Dominic is a born teacher. He is a practical man, discreet, balanced, and grounded. Establishing basic rules, he sketches out a framework within which many others, his sons and followers, will be able to live and follow a path of wisdom. From the beginning, this path of wisdom presents the objective demonstration of his goodness and conviction.

But it would be a mistake to push the characteristics of the two saints to extremes. St. Francis possesses the evangelical wisdom of those who, being "childlike," receive the revelation of the Father (Matt 11:25). St. Dominic is the Spouse of Wisdom. That is to say, he belongs to Christ, whom he contemplates, loves, and serves in simplicity and generosity of heart, in the breadth and fervor of the apostolate, with the same spiritual authenticity as St. Francis; even if their styles, programs, and institutes are different.

For this reason, every evening, after singing Compline and the *Salve Regina*, the Dominicans greet their father and founder with the praise of wisdom.

O Light of the Church (O Lumen Ecclesiae) is intoned by filing out in procession from the church to the choir. The *O Lumen* is a short poem in praise and veneration of Saint Dominic.[3] On the other hand, the responsory *O spem miram* is a poem petitioning St. Dominic and requesting some favor from him. *O lumen*: light of wisdom. To put it another way, that wisdom for which he "was on earth, a splendor of Cherubic light."[4] A mysterious light shone

---

3. "*O lumen Ecclesiae, doctor veritatis, rosa patientiae, ebur castitatis, aquam sapientiae propinasti gratis: praedicator gratiae, nos junge beatis.*" *Horae*, 815. —Trans.

4. Dante, *Paradiso*, 123. —Trans.

physically on his forehead, and it was depicted with a star in the iconography. But the light shone above all in his soul and from him it spread on the earth, so much so that in the *Collect* of his feast it is said: "*Deus qui Ecclesiam tuam Beati Dominici . . .* illuminare *dignatus es meritis et doctrinis . . .* "[5]

Light of the Church. Dominic was not a learned scholar enclosed in the tower of his science and of his intellectual speculation. He was not a man who only shined without illuminating. St. Catherine says of him that he was placed in the Church with the light of knowledge to enlighten. This was his mission, which he transmitted to his Order: to spread the light of the gospel and the light of Christ in the world. Therefore, a very lively *sensus Ecclesiae* flows from him to his Order. Like him, the Order is called to enter the Church with a sapiential function to be fulfilled with "merits and doctrine."

Teacher of Truth (Doctor Veritatis) continues the antiphon. It is a further clarification of the previous affirmation. St. Dominic was not only a scholar, but also a teacher of truth and of life for his own and beyond his Order, for the world and the Church, with his preaching to the people, with the refutation of heretics, and perhaps with the initial spread of the rosary. According to St. Catherine of Siena, in everything, he always exercised the "ministry of the Word." And his Order, in its noblest tradition, has continued this office of representative of the Word, bringing the light of the gospel from one end of the earth to the other with a strong fidelity to the truth.

Rose of Patience (Rosa patientiae). Wisdom is the capacity to sustain the inconveniences that come from things and people in the service of wisdom. Sister Cecilia and the first biographers of St. Dominic bring out these aspects of his personality: patience, kindness, gentleness, and meekness. Patience is the mark of wisdom. Dante says of him: "well disposed toward those he loved."[6]

---

5. From the St. Dominic Missal: "O God, You were pleased to *enlighten* Your Church with the merits and teaching of Blessed Dominic . . . " Intondi, *Saint,* 1051.—Trans.

6. Dante, *Paradiso,* 137.—Trans.

It is the same idea of the invocation "rosa patientiae." But one may wonder whether Dante's other hemistich,[7] "towards his foes severe,"[8] destroys the affirmation of the liturgy. No, "severe" does not have the meaning of "cruel" in Dante's verse, but rather of "unwavering in principles," which does not exclude patience with men, even with the lapsed. "Being both patient and unwavering in principles" is a fruit of wisdom.

Ivory of Chastity (Ebur castitatis). What a virile chastity that of Saint Dominic! It derived from his contemplation of the truth and from his union with wisdom. It was the purity of heart that, while it prepares for contemplation, it also ensues as liberation from earthly images and suggestions by virtue of adherence to the first "intelligible principle."[9] Purity shone in St. Dominic, and it was recommended by him on his deathbed as the secret of effectiveness in the apostolate.

Freely pouring out waters of wisdom (Aquam sapientiae propinasti gratis). Being "light of the Church," "teacher of truth," etc., St. Dominic was able to fulfill his sapiential mission, pouring out the water of wisdom into souls and into the Church, and pouring it "freely." That is to say, pouring it with the right intention, with generosity, without earthly interests, without the jealousy of one who wants to keep the good exclusively to himself. He passed on this spirit and this ideal: to communicate wisdom with joy, with generosity, for the love of truth so consubstantial with the Dominican soul, which because of this does not make too many calculations; and it does not rely upon ambiguous and very comfortable positions.

Preacher of grace unite us with the blessed (Praedicator gratiae, nos iunge beatis). St. Dominic was a "preacher of *grace*" in the Latin and medieval sense of *gratiosus*. He knew how to infuse grace into souls, because he possessed sweetness and anointing. Not unctuousness, because he was full of that gratuitous grace given that is

---

7. An hēmistichium is "a half–line of verse." Glare, "hēmistichium," 790.—Trans.

8. Dante, *Paradiso*, 137. —Trans.

9. Cf. *ST,* II–II, q. 8, a. 7.

the "*sermo sapientiae*" (wise speech), which St. Thomas says is necessary for preachers. Wise speech is necessary in order to: (a) give light to the intelligence of the listener, (b) stir up affections, and (c) move the will to accept what one hears and to practice it. For this purpose, the Lord uses the ministerial and instrumental work of preachers, but the increase comes from the Holy Spirit, who makes the instruments suitable precisely with the "*sermo sapientiae*."[10] This charism penetrated and enlivened the ministry of St. Dominic, making him more a spiritual master than an academic professor and giving the power of the Holy Spirit to the actions he performed by hierarchical mandate in the priestly ministry. Precisely because he was full of this wisdom, he produced so many apostolic achievements in great preaching and in personal encounters.

After this exaltation of the holy patriarch, the conclusion of the antiphon can only be one: unite us with the blessed. It is the prayer that asks for grace to be united to the blessed in the same sense as the "*O Spem miram*." After having served wisdom on earth, one asks to be admitted to participate in and enjoy the triumph of wisdom in heaven. It is the grace of a "happy death" that the servants of wisdom ask of their father and bridegroom of wisdom.

10. Cf. *ST*, II–II, q. 177, a. 1.

Chapter 16

From Beatitudes to Beatitude

TRUE WISDOM HAS GOD, from whom it descends, as its ultimate end (cf. Jas 3:17). It is a participation in the wisdom of God[1] that allows man to realize, already in the present life, knowledge of God and of things similar to that which God has in himself. That is to say, it allows him to have ordered knowledge, albeit manifold, but focused only on the one thing necessary, although divided among numerous concepts and analogies, fixed in the eternal, even if subject to the variety of things that flow over time.

By virtue of wisdom, already in the present life, one reaches something eternal in knowledge and leads to the perfection of human knowledge itself, and the faculty of the intellect is fully actualized. As St. Thomas teaches, universal and perfect judgment on things cannot be obtained except by relating them to the ultimate cause, as wisdom does.[2]

Also, action proceeds ordered and charged with eternal value from the spiritual perfection reached in contemplation through wisdom. "Divine things are indeed necessary and eternal in themselves, yet they are the rules of the contingent things which are the subject-matter of human actions."[3]

---

1. *ST*, II–II, q. 23, a. 2, ad 1.
2. *ST*, I–II, q. 67, a. 2.
3. *ST*, II–II, q. 45, a. 3, ad 2.

To wisdom belongs first of all the contemplation of divine things, which is a vision of principles for "the direction of human acts according to Divine rules."[4]

On the other hand, false wisdom, the "wisdom of the age," bad and foolish, is that which chooses as an end a worldly good.[5] But precisely for this reason it is a real foolishness by which man, by plunging himself into earthly things, loses the sense of the eternal and so empties the value of his thought and life.[6]

Unfortunately, earthly life takes place amid the continuous conflict between wisdom and folly, as experience and history teach. Everything depends on the end that is chosen and that is proposed as the cornerstone of life, as the reason for everything.

The truly wise pre-selects the eternal goal, that is, God in whom is true bliss. The Christian knows that it is a reachable goal in the celestial glory through the development of grace, which is its seed and beginning.[7] In correspondence to the ultimate end and as concrete realization of grace, acts of supernatural virtues, and especially those of the most exquisite and perfect ones that are called beatitudes, approach Beatitude. And indeed they already carry something in themselves as an immanent reward to the practice of virtues, of which they are the perfect exercise.[8]

It is an anticipated beatitude, a merit that contains, in *essence*, the prize, namely "an imperfect inchoation of future happiness in holy men, even in this life," as in a tree that is not only green with leaves (*virescit frondibus*) but already offers the first produce of fruits (*primordia fructuum*).[9] On the basis of these first fruits, of these anticipations of beatitude in man who progresses in the exercise of the virtues and the gifts of the Holy Spirit, one can hope that

4. *ST*, II–II, q. 45, a. 3, ad 3.
5. *ST*, II–II, q. 46, a. 1, ad 2.
6. *ST*, II–II, q. 46, a. 2.
7. *ST*, I–II, q. 69, a. 2.
8. *ST*, I–II, q. 69, a. 1, ad 3.
9. *ST*, I–II, q. 69, a. 2.

he will come to "perfection as a citizen of the heavenly kingdom,"[10] as the first fruits that establish the hope of the harvest.

And here are the series of beatitudes that according to Jesus are already in this life beginnings and morsels of heavenly bliss:

The kingdom of heaven as the beginning of perfect wisdom in those in whom the kingdom of the spirit is affirmed.

The possession of the earth as stability of soul in the possession of the divine inheritance.

The consolation that the Holy Spirit, who is the Paraclete (or Comforter), gives to those who subject themselves to the promptings of the Spirit.

The mercy of God granted even in this life to those who exercise mercy.

The vision of God anticipated in an obscure way in those who have the eye of the mind purified by the gift of understanding.

The divine sonship realized in interior peace when man possesses in himself order according to the exigencies of true wisdom, which makes everything converge in God.

All are initial beatitudes, however, whose perfection will be had only *in patria* (in the heavenly homeland).[11] Here on the way (*in via*), they are limited and imperfect, but they mark an entire itinerary of spiritual life, which under the direction and inspiration of wisdom develops in beatitude and leads to its fullness.

One can perhaps trace a certain pattern of their roles in the economy of the path of perfection, on the basis of the list given to us by St. Matthew.

A first group of beatitudes refers to the victory over the hedonistic life, which according to the worldly spirit constitutes, for many, happiness; and this alleged happiness is instead an impediment in the path to celestial beatitude. So to overcome what concerns riches and earthly honors, the beatitude of poverty is given; to deal with aggressive passions, meekness is given; and to battle against passions tending towards pleasure, the beatitude

10. *ST*, I–II, q. 69, a. 2.
11. Cf. *ST*, I–II, q. 69, a. 2, ad 3.

about weeping is given, because it is a sign and effect of the spirit of penitence and mortification.

The second group is that of the beatitudes of the active life: in giving to our neighbor according to what is due to him, the thirst for justice is given; and in giving him freely, in the form of spontaneous benefits, the beatitude of mercy is given.

The third group includes the beatitudes of the contemplative life, and that is the final and perfect beatitude. One merits this beatitude with the results of the active life, namely purity and *peace*, and the inchoative beatitude, which is above all a work of wisdom that is rewarded with the vision of God and with divine sonship.

The beatitudes, in fact, both as merit and reward, correspond to the gifts of the Holy Spirit and depend on them: divine sonship and peace correspond to wisdom; the vision of God and purity correspond to understanding; consolation and weeping correspond to knowledge; mercy corresponds to counsel; fulfillment as a reward for the thirst for justice corresponds to piety; the possession of the earth as a reward to meekness corresponds to fortitude; and the kingdom of God as a reward to poverty corresponds to the fear of the Lord.

Whatever may be the value of these connections established by St. Thomas,[12] one thing is certain, and it is that the gospel beatitudes represent a reversal of the usual criteria and systems of appraisal of things in vogue in the world. They represent an aspiration towards the renewal of spirit and life, mentality and custom, which is illuminated towards heavenly perfection.

The same correlation between merit and the reward contained in each of the gospel beatitudes allows us to better define the function that the beatitudes, as a whole, play in the spiritual life.

As for the victory over worldly pleasures and the abandonment of the life that is overcome, here are three degrees: (1) the abandonment of earthly things gives way to poverty as merit and to the possession of the kingdom of God as a reward; (2) the abandonment of quarrels and secular disputes gives way to meekness as merit and to the possession of the earth as a reward; and (3) the abandonment

12. See *ST*, I–II, q. 69, a. 2, ad 3 and a. 4.

of worldly concupiscence gives way to weeping, or penitence, and merit and consolation as a reward.

In the active life, the victory over injustice that is often committed by greed over earthly goods gives way to "thirst for justice" as merit and to the satiety of good as a reward; and the well—regulated fulfillment of the works of mercy obtains divine mercy.

In the contemplative life, the reward of the vision of God corresponds to the merit of interior purity; to the merit of purification, carried out to be more like God, corresponds the "glory of Divine sonship, consisting in perfect union with God through consummate wisdom" (*per sapientiam consummatam*).[13]

And yet, the beatitudes are not Beatitude. They give us a foretaste of it and together they kindle in the soul, which is more and more alive, the desire for heaven.

This tendency is in the immanent dynamic of the virtues and the gifts of the Holy Spirit. Faith is striving towards the glory of the divine vision. Hope is striving towards the full and stable possession of God. Charity is striving towards perfect communion with God. The moral virtues strive to reach perfect celestial harmony.[14] And the gifts of the Holy Spirit strive to bring about a subjugation, an adherence, a total docility of the soul to the Holy Spirit.

Heaven, as we represent and call it according to our way of imagining and speaking, the future vision, and the future possession of God in light and love, will be realized in the soul through the "light of glory" and charity. But this essential bliss, consisting of communion with God, will not exclude but will strengthen and exalt the spiritual values achieved on earth. It will strengthen and exalt the spiritual value of the virtues by which the order of reason, harmony, and beauty will be made perfect. It will strengthen and exalt the gifts of the Holy Spirit, whose formal element, that is, ductility under the action of the Holy Spirit (*mobilitas a Spiritu Sancto*), will achieve its perfect fulfillment when "God will be all in all" (1 Cor 15:28), and man will be completely subjected to him. The values of the beatitudes will then have its fullness in beatitude.

13. *ST*, I–II, q. 69, a. 4.
14. *ST*, I–II, q. 67, a. 5.

In particular, wisdom will then be consummated in perfect divine sonship and actuated in the beatific vision. This will be the true beatitude in which life in wisdom will mature and find a transcendent conclusion: knowledge, certainty of possession, eternal contemplation, and the new taste of God.

The virtues and the gifts of the Holy Spirit will no longer have to be exercised in relation to the matter that was proper to them on earth, namely the practice of the good according to reason and according to the Holy Spirit in the various fields of human life. This phase of experimentation and exercise will be over by then. Their essence, their psychological—ethical value will instead be the supreme expression of human perfection in the glory of God communicated to the soul.

The beatitudes will no longer include the component of merit, because the time for works will be finished. The trial period will be finished. On the other hand, the component of the reward that they contain will be dilated and founded in the only beatitude of communion with God, in whom the "kingdom," the "possession of the land," "the vision of God," the "consolation," the "mercy," the "satiety" of the good, in short all the evangelical promises, will have their perfect actuation.

Wisdom will no longer flourish in a shadowy contemplation, as if almost vespertine,[15] although sapid and joyous, as it is that which always takes place in the context of faith. But it will be identified with the light of the divine vision, with the vital participation in the eternal generation of the divine idea, the Word, and in the contemplation of the divine persons spirating love and bound in love.

Life in wisdom on earth is illuminated by the infinite splendor of that eternal life of Trinitarian contemplation, which is already

15. The term was introduced by St. Augustine (IV Super Gen. c. 22, ML 34, 311–312), and recovered and explained by St. Thomas (*ST*, I, q. 58, a. 6), to designate cognition that the angels have of the being of things not in the Word (*cognitio matutina*) but in their very nature. However, the distinction can also be applied to the way of knowing God, in himself or in things, proper of the human soul in the different states in which it finds herself: in this or in the next life. See also *DV*, q. 8, a. 16.

participated in a germinal and inchoative way for those who believe in Christ (John 3:26; 6:40, 47; 20:31, etc.); and it is nourished by his body and his blood. In other words, they participate in it by supernatural spirituality, by grace, and by all the divine gifts that it brings to man with his redemptive work. His redemptive work is renewed in the eucharistic mystery. This is how one has, in what St. Theresa called the "little heaven of the soul," a reflection of divine beatitude, a beginning of eternal life (the beginning of glory, *inchoatio beatitudinis*),[16] a divine transformation of the whole human being, and indeed an indwelling of God in the soul.[17]

There is no doubt that for those who believe, for those who love the Lord, this seating at the banquet of wisdom, sacramentalized in the Eucharist ("wisdom has spread her table": Prov 9:2, as written by St. Thomas in the office of *Corpus Domini*), is the secret of happiness that, even amid penumbra and the vicissitudes and the trials of the present life, is already given to enjoy down here in the enclosure. This banquet of wisdom here on earth is more interior than exterior, where contemplation and prayer flourish, in that climate of recollection; and where the soul knows the peace that the world cannot give or take away (John 14:27), and that Christ grants as beatitude to the one who lives as a child of God.

16. *ST*, II–II, q. 24, a. 3 ad 2.
17. *ST*, I, q. 43, a. 3.

Bibliography

Aquinas, Thomas. "De Veritate." In *S. Thomae Aquinatis Quaestiones Disputatae Editio VIII*. vol. 1. Edited by Raimondo Spiazzi. Turin, Italy: Marietti, 1949.

———. *The Summa Contra Gentiles of Saint Thomas Aquinas*, vol.1. Translated by the English Dominican Fathers from the Latest Leonine Edition. London: Burns, Oates & Washbourne, 1924.

———. *Summa Theologiae: First Complete American Edition*. Translated by Fathers of the English Dominican Province. New York: Benziger, 1947.

Aristotle. *The Athenian Constitution; The Eudemian Ethics; On Virtues and Vices*. Translated by Harris Rackham. Loeb Classical Library 285. Rev. ed. London: W. Heinemann, 1952.

Berthier, Joachim J. ed. *Humberti de Romanis Opera De Vita Regulari*, vol. 2. Torino: Marietti, 1956.

Britt, Matthew, ed. *The Hymns of the Breviary and Missal*. Rev. ed. New York: Benziger Brothers, 1922.

Brooks, Darlene L. "Archeology of Early Christianity in Egypt." In *The Oxford Handbook of Early Christian Archeology*, edited by William R. Caraher et al., 665–84. Oxford: Oxford University Press, 2019. https://doi.org/10.1093/oxfordhb/9780199369041.013.21

Dalmases, Candido D., ed. *Obras Completas de San Ignacio de Loyola*. Madrid: Biblioteca de Autores Cristianos, 1963.

Dante Alighieri. *The Divine Comedy of Dante Alighieri, vol. 1: Inferno*. Translated by Courtney Langdon. Cambridge: Harvard University Press, 1918.

———. *The Divine Comedy of Dante Alighieri, vol. 3: Paradiso*. Translated by Courtney Langdon. Cambridge: Harvard University Press, 1921.

———. *The Divine Comedy of Dante Alighieri, vol. 2: Purgatorio*. Translated by Courtney Langdon. Cambridge: Harvard University Press, 1920.

Dominicans. *The Book of Constitutions and Ordinations of the Brothers of the Order of Preachers*. Published by order of Br. Carlos Aspiroz A. Costa, Master of the Order. Dublin: Dominican, 2012.

Glare, Peter G.W. ed. "hēmistichium" In *OLD* 790. New York: Oxford University Press, 1982.

———. "Opto." In *OLD* 1260. New York: Oxford University Press, 1982.

Horae Diurnae: Juxta Ritum Sacri Ordinis Praedicatorum, Apostolicam Auctoritate Approbatum. Jussu editae. Romae: S. Sabinae, 1956.

Intondi, Urban P. *The Saint Dominic Missal, Latin-English.* 1st ed. New York: Saint Dominic Missal, 1959.

Jackson, Charles J. "Something that happened to me at Manresa." *Studies in the Spirituality of Jesuits* 38.2 (2006) 1–40. https://ejournals.bc.edu/index.php/jesuit/issue/view/509

Liturgia Horarum: Iuxta Ritum Romanum. Editio typical altera. Vol. 3. Ed. Città del Vaticano: Libreria Editrice Vaticana, 2000.

Maritain, Jacques. "On Knowledge through Connaturality." *The Review of Metaphysics* 4.4 (1951) 473–81.

Molinaro, Aniceto. "La Neoscolastica Italiana." *Rivista di Filosofia Neo-Scolastica* 82.2/3 (1990) 436–54. https://www.jstor.org/stable/43063302.

Mountain, William J., ed. *Sancti Aurelii Augustini De Trinitate Libri XV.* Corpus Christianorum Series Latine L.Turnholti, Turnhout, Belgium: Typographi Brepols, 1968.

Lilla, Salvatore and Claudio Moreschini, ed. *Dionysii Areopagitae De Divinis Nominibus.* Hellenica 71. Alessandria: Edizioni dell'Orso, 2018.

Roest, Bert. "The Franciscan Hermit: Seeker, Prisoner, Refugee." *Church History and Religious Culture* 86.1/4 (2006) 163–89. https://www.jstor.org/stable/23922515

Rule, Martin, ed. *The Missal of St. Augustine's Abbey Canterbury with Excerpts from the Antiphonary and Lectionary of the Same Monastery.* Cambridge: Cambridge University Press, 1896.

Sedlmayr, Hans. *Art in Crisis: The Lost of the Center.* Translated by Brian Battershaw. New York: Routledge, 2006.

Somida Awad, Hind Salah El-Din. "Some Aspects of Monastic Diets from Thebes: A Comparative Study of the Consumption of Fish and Meat." *Scrinium* 16.1 (2020) 48–57. https://doi.org/10.1163/18177565-00161P05

Spiers, Alexander G.H. "'Vita Nuova' and 'Dolce Stil Nuovo.'" *Modern Languages Notes* 25.2 (1910) 37–39. https://doi:10.2307/2916306

Zimmerman, Carle C. "American Roots in an Italian Village." *Genus* 11.1/4 (1955) 78–139. http://www.jstor.org/stable/29787233